Encouragement

Melinda Doljac

WESTBOW
PRESS
A DIVISION OF THOMAS NELSON

WestBow Press books may be ordered through booksellers or by contacting:

WestBow Press
A Division of Thomas Nelson
1663 Liberty Drive
Bloomington, IN 47403
www.westbowpress.com
1-(866) 928-1240

ISBN: 978-1-4497-4124-2 (hc)
ISBN: 978-1-4497-4123-5 (sc)
ISBN: 978-1-4497-4122-8 (e)

Library of Congress Control Number: 2012903202

Printed in the United States of America

WestBow Press rev. date: 03/07/2012

Contents

I would like to thank my two girls and my son in law for all of their help. Rachel, Rusty and Lana

Chapter 1

There Is a Difference between a Christian and a Saint

The book of Psalms tells us a "saint" is one who sings praises to the Lord, gives thanks, and is preserved by the Lord—a true follower of Jesus Christ.

The worst enemy of a saint is a Christian. This is a bold statement, but it's true. I have seen it over and over again. Let's take the workplace for an example. When a saint is around a Christian, the saint works very hard at his job—not to please the employer, but to please the Lord. The saint is a model employee because he is trying to be a reflection of Christ every moment of every day.

The Christian coworker sees how the saint is working and acting. The Christian knows that he is in error in his behavior because he sees the saint's conduct. This often makes the Christian turn against the saint. It's quite ironic, and unfortunately I've seen it many times.

A Christian is still living in the world or may even have just one foot in the world. But this isn't how the Lord instructs His followers to be. He wants our actions to glorify Him, as we claim to others we believe in Him. How are cursing, listening to and telling dirty jokes, lying, being selfish, deceiving, name-calling, getting drunk, and premarital sex glorifying the Lord?

I often hear, "Oh, the Lord understands." Does He really? According to Scripture, God does not understand. In fact He tells us over and over again that these people are condemned because their lives have not changed to be reflections of Christ. They do not bear good fruit. They go against the Ten Commandments and refuse to repent.

> You will know them by their fruits. Do men gather grapes from thornbushes or figs from thistles? Even so, every good tree bears good fruit, but a bad tree bears bad fruit. (Matthew 7:16-17)

> Do you not know that the unrighteous will not inherit the kingdom of God? Do not be deceived. Neither fornicators, nor idolaters, nor adulterers, nor homosexuals, nor sodomites, nor thieves, nor covetous, nor drunkards, nor revilers, nor extortioners will inherit the kingdom of God. (1 Corinthians 6:9-10)

> Idolatry, sorcery, hatred, contentions, jealousies, outbursts of wrath, selfish ambitions, dissensions, heresies, envy, murders, drunkenness, revelries and the like; of which I tell you beforehand, just as I also told you in time past, that those who practice such things will not inherit the kingdom of God. (Galatians 5:20-21)

These verses are straight from the Lord! Whoever says that the Lord understands his sinful life does not know God or His commandments. This person, whether he means to or not, is glorifying Satan with his actions. The Lord wants us to be pure and holy; He wants us to serve Him and not ourselves and the world. We are to love Him more than the air that we breathe, more than the next heartbeat.

So how do you make the transition to being the saint that the Lord takes pride in? You can start by praying without ceasing (1 Thessalonians 5:17). This is a great way to get closer to the Lord. People see this verse and overlook it, though, because they think it's impossible. It isn't. If you ask the Holy Spirit to help you train yourself to pray constantly, to stay in constant communication with the Lord, after a couple of weeks it will be as natural as breathing. You'll also find yourself much closer to the Lord.

You want to change your perception and how you see things. You want to develop what I call "spiritual eyes," eyes that the Lord would see the world from. Pray and ask the Holy Spirit for His help to close your worldly eyes and look out of "spiritual eyes." You will see everything differently. It will change your life completely! When you look around a room, you'll be able to see what is really going on spiritually. Dirty jokes, slander—it all takes on a new meaning. Being able to constantly see like this takes practice, but with the help of the Holy Spirit, you can perfect it. You'll never go back to looking through worldly eyes again. The Lord will surely use you more.

Remember, we are not of this world. So it's only reasonable that we don't see and perceive things the way nonbelievers do.

> If you were of the world, the world would love its own. Yet because you are not of the world, but

> I chose you out of the world, therefore the world
> hates you. (John 15:19)

Does the world hate you? Do people talk about you negatively because of the way you live your life for the Lord? Then praise the Lord! You are living this verse. The Lord will be glorified by you and you will be used greatly by Him.

Being very different from nonbelievers is hard, and any bit of encouragement helps. Of course there are many sources of encouragement in the Bible. One verse I find particularly helpful comes from Philippians.

> For our citizenship is in heaven, from which we also
> eagerly wait for the Savior, the Lord Jesus Christ,
> who will transform our lowly body that it may be
> conformed to His glorious body, according to the
> working by which He is able even to subdue all
> things to Himself. (Philippians 3:20-21)

I volunteer in a nursing home by giving "spiritual support" to patients. I have patients who tell me that they just want to go home. I tell them, "So do I." Along with others, I bring them those passages from Philippians that state our home is with Christ Jesus in heaven. When He's ready for us, He will bring us home to be with Him. What a glorious day that will be!

A saint is to live his life as if running a race, with Jesus our Lord at the finish line. We hunger to hear the words from our Lord at the end of the race: "Come, you blessed of My Father; inherit the kingdom prepared for you from the foundation of the world" (Matthew 25:34).

I have had people say to me that it's easy for me to see things differently and not be worldly, because I'm "elected." But I assure you that the Lord gave *all* of us the choice—the free will—to go down any road that we want! I have chosen the road to serve the almighty God, and you can too.

Don't use your weakness and desire for worldliness to justify not following the Lord. Look to Scripture and see how the Lord will accept *anyone*! "I love those who love me, and those who seek me diligently will find me" (Proverbs 8:17). This includes you!

> Ask, and it will be given to you; seek, and you will find; knock, and it will be opened to you. For everyone who asks receives, and he who seeks finds, and to him who knocks it will be opened. (Matthew 7:7-8)

In these verses, Jesus says "everyone." Not some elected people, but everyone! You have to pray; you have to repent.

Note the word "repent" doesn't mean that you ask forgiveness for your sins and the next day do it all over again. "Repent" means to ask for forgiveness of your sins with all of your heart and never—yes, I said never—go back to your sins again. You may say that you believe in the Lord and love Him with all of your heart. But the Lord finds words cheap. You must prove your love for the Lord like Jesus did.

Pray and read the Scripture every day. This can take great effort, but take heart in the fact that you're being obedient. Before reading the word of God, ask the Holy Spirit to help you, and He will. "The Helper, the Holy Spirit, whom the Father will send in My name, He will teach you all things" (John 14:26).

Lean on the Holy Spirit to give you understanding. Let Him help you. Don't just read the words. You must live what you read. If you prove to the Lord that you aren't just all talk, that you really want to change and live for Him, He will gladly open up the door.

"Behold, I stand at the door and knock. If anyone hears My voice and opens the door, I will come in to him and dine with him, and he with Me" (Revelation 3:20). Just the fact that you are reading this book tells me that the Lord is trying to get your attention—He is knocking. It's up to you. You can say, as the prophets have in the past and as the Lord's saints do now, "*Here I am, Lord!*"

> Then the Angel of God spoke to me in a dream, saying, "Jacob." And I said, "Here I am." (Genesis 31:11)

> So when the Lord saw that he turned aside to look, God called to him from the midst of the bush and said, "Moses, Moses!"

> And he said, "Here I am." (Exodus 3:4)

> Now there was a certain disciple at Damascus named Ananias; and to him the Lord said in a vision, "Ananias."

> And he said, "Here I am, Lord." (Acts 9:10)

Acts 8:26-31 also shows us how the Lord still speaks to us today. We just have to be right with the Lord and ready and hungry enough to listen. Maybe He's not calling you in a vision; maybe He's sending His Holy Spirit to get your attention. As with Ananias, you have to say: "*Here I am, Lord.*" Learn from Saul, who kept refusing to open the door that the Lord was knocking on.

And he said, "Who are You Lord?" Then the Lord said, "I am Jesus, whom you are persecuting. It *is* hard for you to kick against the goads." (Acts 9:5)

Is He saying this to you? Are you persecuting the Lord with your sinful life by ignoring the knocking at the door? Is He telling you it *is* hard for you to kick against the goads? Let me explain what this means.

The goad is a long stick with a pin or a pointed spike attached. The farmer used the goad to make his cattle or oxen move. In this verse, the goad means "against the Lord." So the Lord is telling Saul that he is only hurting himself by kicking against the Lord.

Are you kicking against the goad by constantly ignoring the sound of the Lord knocking on your door? Here are a couple verses of encouragement that I like:

I sought the Lord and He heard me, and delivered me from all my fears. (Psalm 34:4)

It is better to trust in the Lord than to put confidence in man. (Psalm 118:8)

The bottom line is, whom do you serve? God or Satan? Do you live to please the Lord with everything you do and say, or do you live in the world? There isn't any in-between. The person who proclaims to be a Christian has to be aware of this. A Christian's biggest fear is to reach the afterlife only to have the Lord say to him, "I never knew you."

Many will say to Me in that day, "Lord, Lord have we not prophesied in Your name, cast out demons in Your name and done many wonders in Your name?" And then I will declare to them, "I never knew you;

depart from Me, you who practice lawlessness."
(Matthew 7:22-23)

Consider whether or not the Lord knows you now like He wants to know you. As you seek to know the Lord more, remember to be cautious of what other people say is in the Bible. They are only human and can be wrong. Read the Word of God alone, and, with the help of the Holy Spirit, you will understand it fully and live a life that is pleasing to the Lord.

> And Jabez called on God of Israel saying, "Oh, that You would bless me indeed, and enlarge my territory, that Your hand would be with me, and that You would keep *me* from evil that I may not cause pain!" (1 Choronicles 4:10)

Here Jabez is knocking and asking the Lord to expand his territory of service to the Lord. He also asks the Lord to use him better. The Lord granted Jabez the request, and He will do the same for you.

Please remember that it's false to think that just because you believe in Jesus you have a free ticket to heaven, that you belong to Him. Satan also believes in Jesus.

Chapter 2

How Do You Serve?

As followers of Jesus, we always want to stay in the church and enjoy the fellowship of other Christians. We go to as many Bible studies as we can just to enjoy the presence of other Christians, people like us. Then, when we are out in the world, we become part of the world and never practice what we learn in all the classes we attend. Everything that is taught goes in one ear and out the other, but we enjoy the fellowship while we're there. Sometimes I'll ask people what they're learning in their Bible study and what they do with the information. The answer never seems to be the most important one: that they share their knowledge with others. When I ask them how they can use their knowledge from their Bible study to witness for the Lord, they look at me blankly.

Staying active in church, making it every Sunday, and staying dedicated to Bible studies are excellent ways of staying in touch with other Christians and learning more and more about the faith the Lord wants you to share. But are you going to all of the Bible studies just to benefit yourself? Just to make yourself feel happy and accomplished? Is it all about you and your fellowship with your friends? Is the Bible in the background?

I'm not saying that it's wrong to enjoy fellowshipping with other Christians. We all need the encouragement. But there is a time and a place for having fun with other Christians and it isn't in Bible study.

Bible study is about learning how to serve the Lord in the world. You need to be equipped with solid doctrine as a suit of armor for our battle on the front lines for our Lord. He should be able to use us as His warriors, armed with the knowledge we gather from our studies.

> But be doers of the word and not hearers only, deceiving yourselves. (James 1:22)

Are you learning as much as you can from morning service and Bible studies? Can you go out into the world and serve the Lord with what you have learned? Can you go to the front lines of the battlefield and try the best you can to be a warrior for our Lord? Can you encourage and counsel people that the Lord brings to you during the week? Can you try as hard as you can to be used by the Lord as His tool to expand His kingdom on earth as well as in heaven? Do you go to Bible study to be able to do these things? I hope so.

Chapter 3

You Want to Serve the Lord but Don't Know How

You want to serve the Lord but don't know how. The first thing I would suggest is to learn as much of the Word of God as you can. Listen to the services your pastor prepares. Go to as many Bible studies as you can, and read the Bible from cover to cover over and over and over again. You can do it; there is no doubt in my mind. Never stop reading the written word. Don't just read the word, but live what you read. We have to live what we read!

The Lord gave us the Bible so that a child could understand it. You don't need self-proclaimed prophets or rabbis to tell you what the Word of God says. They are only human, and they can be wrong, just like you and I can be wrong.

You must read the Word daily and pray as often as you can throughout the day. You'll be in sync with the Lord, and you'll see and understand when the Lord instructs you in the way you should serve Him.

> I am the vine, you *are* the branches. He who abides
> in Me, and I in him, bears much fruit; for without
> Me you can do nothing. (John 15:5)

> He who says he abides in Him ought himself also to
> walk just as He walked. (1 John 2:6)

Pray, pray, pray for the Holy Spirit to help you understand what you're reading. Then, live what you read. The writings of the Bible are not just for the people of that time: they are for all of us.

> I will instruct you and teach you in the way you
> should go; I will guide you with My eye. (Psalm
> 32:8)

I love this verse, and it is so true. This verse keeps me going. Whenever I see the Lord leading me down an unknown path, someplace where I wouldn't go on my own, I automatically ask the Lord, "Why am I here, Lord?"

When I'm stuck next to someone who makes me uncomfortable, but they try to talk to me, I ask the Lord, "Why is this person trying to talk to me?" Clearly, if they want to talk to me, I know that the Lord placed that person by me so the Lord can be glorified through me. I know that He is with me always, and He'll instruct me as a puppet on a string. He'll use me as His tool. Praise the Lord!

Before the Lord lifts you up to a higher level of service for Him, He might put you through some *really* hard trials. If this is what you experience, don't ask anyone to pray you out of those trials! Let the Lord totally break you down to nothing. It can be a horrible ordeal and last for a while. But don't pray yourself out of those trials, and don't have anyone pray you out of those trials until the Lord lets it be known that the time is over. If you would be prayed out of the trials, then you would end up being a half-made vessel for the Lord. You won't be used like He wants to use you.

When you endure the trials of a total breakdown, the Lord will be able to use you as a new child in Christ—as a brand-new tool for Him to use to expand His kingdom. Here are some encouraging verses:

> But may the God of all grace, who called us to His eternal glory by Christ Jesus, after you have suffered a while, perfect, establish, strengthen, and settle *you*. (1 Peter 5:10)

> Cast your burden on the LORD, and He shall sustain you: He shall never permit the righteous to be moved. (Psalm 55:22)

> Blessed *is* the man who endures temptation; for when he has been approved, he will receive the crown of life which the Lord has promised to those who love Him. (James 1:12)

> But He knows the way that I take; *When* He has tested me, I shall come forth as gold. My foot has held fast to His steps; I have kept His way and not turned aside. (Job 23:10-11)

> Beloved, do not think it strange concerning the fiery trial which is to try you, as though some strange thing happened to you; but rejoice to the extent that you partake of Christ's sufferings, that when His glory is revealed, you may also be glad with exceeding joy. (1 Peter 4:12-13)

> Yet if *anyone suffers* as a Christian, let him not be ashamed, but let him glorify God in this matter. (1 Peter 4:16)

Being a saint is much more than just a wonderful relationship with the Lord. When we finally reach this level, we have to look through our "spiritual eyes" to see where the Lord wants us to go in order that he may use us.

I have seen so many people who see that the Lord has an open door for them to walk through to serve Him. I have seen these saints use their free will and refuse to go through that door, refuse to serve the Lord where He sends them. They in turn are telling the Lord, "No Lord, it's not me, and I don't want to do that type of service. I'm just not comfortable going there."

Yes, you have your free will, but if you refuse and say no to the Lord, then you will have to suffer the consequences. These consequences can be very, very severe. Even after I pleaded with them, I know saints who have refused to stay on the Lord's path, and they suffered the negative consequences.

Turning down the Lord is very dangerous. He may never use us again, and that idea should be like a dagger going through your heart.

Even though the Lord may lead us down a road out of our comfort zone, we must always remember: who are we to please and who do we serve? Do we serve the Lord or ourselves? Whenever we see the Lord take notice of us and give us the privilege to serve Him, we must be prepared to go outside of our comfort zone! We must run, not walk, through that door as fast as we can. If we go too slowly, the door might close and the opportunity will be gone.

He will give us the strength, knowledge, and wisdom we need to be a service to Him. We are assured that we are not going through that door alone: the Lord is going through it with us. He will put the words in our minds and tell us what to say; He will bring other saints to help us along. He will teach us what we need to know; He will lead us and guide us. We just need to have the desire to serve Him and a deep faith. We must have the hunger and the passion to serve Him wherever He leads us, as unfamiliar and scary the roads ahead might be. Then the Lord will use us beyond our imagination for His honor and glory.

In turn, after your trial is over, He will bring you into new, greater seasons of service, where you can use what you have learned. I like the following verse; it's a parable that stands true in our service to our Lord:

> His lord said to him, "Well *done*, good and faithful servant: you have been faithful over a few things, I will make you ruler over many things. Enter into the joy of your lord." (Matthew 25:23)

This is so true as long as we run through the open door and serve Him with all that we have and never say no to the Lord.

Chapter 4

Let Us Talk about Prayer

What is prayer? Prayer is the communication between man and God. Some people think that prayer needs to be structured so they can repeat words without thinking: short and sweet, only done at night before bed, or only if they have a need.

I spent some time in a couple of Jewish synagogues in order to observe their beliefs. Before they began to study the Torah (the first five books of the Old Testament), they would always pray the same structured prayer:

Blessed is the Eternal, our God, ruler of the universe, who hallows us with mitzvoth [laws] and commands us to engage in the study of Torah.

This is said in Hebrew before the study. Some of the people had no idea what they were saying, but they were perfectly content memorizing the prayer to God. When they pray, they do so as fast as they can, just to get it over with. I firmly believe this is wrong. This thoughtlessness is a consequence of following the teachings and traditions of man and not the teachings of God through His written word.

> And when you pray, do not use vain repetitions
> as the heathen *do*. For they think that they will be
> heard for their many words. (Matthew 6:7)

I believe that when we pray, we are to pray to our Lord with all our hearts. We are to pray with words from our hearts—with sincerity, love, and respect.

Prayer is a way for us to communicate with God, a way for us to ask our Lord for help. It's a way to thank the Lord for what He's doing in our lives, even for the food He has provided for us to eat.

The Lord tells us and shows us throughout Scripture that we are to pray. He shows us how to pray, as well as when and where to pray, beginning with the book of Genesis and ending with Revelation.

There is a verse that comes to mind in the book of Hebrews that I really like.

> Let us therefore come boldly to the throne of grace,
> that we may obtain mercy and find grace to help in
> time of need. (Hebrews 4:16)

To the throne of grace! How thankful we should be for the throne of grace. When you pray, do you close your eyes and picture the throne of the Lord? When you pray, it's good to go to a room all by yourself and close the door. Jesus says:

> When you pray, you shall not be like the hypocrites.
> For they love to pray standing in the synagogues
> and on the corners of the streets, that they may be
> seen by men. Assuredly, I say to you, they have their
> reward. But you, when you pray, go into your room
> and when you have shut your door, pray to your

Father who *is* in the secret *place*; and your Father who sees in secret will reward you openly. And when you pray, do not use vain repetitions as the heathen *do*. For they think that they will be heard for their many words. (Matthew 6:5-7)

When you are in your room and ready to pray, ask the Holy Spirit to help you to pray.

Likewise the Spirit also helps in our weaknesses. For we do not know what we should pray for as we ought, but the Spirit Himself makes intercession for us with groanings which cannot be uttered. Now He who searches the hearts knows what the mind of the Spirit *is*, because He makes intercession for the saints according to *the will of God*. (Romans 8:26-27)

Also, when you are asking the Holy Spirit to help you to pray, ask Him to bring you up to the throne room of the Lord. Close your eyes and picture the face of Jesus and ask the Holy Spirit to bring you into the throne room, into the presence of the Lord. Then as you concentrate on Jesus, you will be in the presence of the Father. Pray with all of your heart.

True prayer is the Spirit of God's approach to the soul, thereby bringing it to the throne of God. It is not a mental exercise or a vocal performance, but it is deeper: it is a spiritual communication with the Creator of heaven and earth.

The work of the Holy Spirit is needed. The Holy Spirit himself must be present all through the prayer; He will help us to pray, to give life and power to our prayers.

The intercession of the Lord Jesus Christ is essential to acceptable prayer. A prayer is not truly a prayer without the

Spirit of God, and it will not prevail without the Son of God. He, the Great High Priest, must go within the veil for us.

Prayer should always be regarded as an entrance into the courts of heaven, and we must approach our prayer with *complete submission.*

We are called to the throne of *grace,* not to the throne of law. Grace apprehended sin. Beneath the burden, grace carried sin up to the cross and nailed it there, slew it there, put it to death forever, and triumphed gloriously.

Grace sits on a throne because it has conquered human sin! Grace has borne the penalty of human guilt and has overthrown all its enemies.

Grace, moreover, sits on the throne because it has established itself there *by right.* There is no injustice in the grace of God.

What a wonderful privilege the Lord has given us, to enable us to come unto the throne of grace to pray to almighty God, with the help of the Holy Spirit and the intercession of our Lord Jesus Christ.

When you pray, never stop concentrating upon the Lord. Here are suggestions for your prayer time.

> ➤ Give the Lord honor, praise Him, bless Him, and give Him glory because He is deserving.
> ➤ Then, thank Him for everything He is doing in your life and for answered prayers.
> ➤ Tell Him how much He means to you—bless the Lord with everything you have. Then give Him any concerns that you have on your heart.
> ➤ Then intercede for your loved ones—friends, ministries, your pastor, and the government.

> ➢ Then thank the Lord for the wonderful time of prayer: for the closeness, for allowing you to be in His presence, for accepting your prayers, and for His answers. Prayer is so special and God finds delight in your honest prayers.

There are also those short prayers. For instance, there are prayers you'll often hear before a meal. Don't let these prayers be routine and mindless! Close your eyes and concentrate upon the Lord and pray with all of your heart for the meal He has provided. Ask Him to bless the food and the conversations if you're with others.

Let us never forget this very special verse from 1 Thessalonians: "Pray without ceasing." As I mentioned before, people often overlook this verse. People think that this is impossible, but it isn't! If you love the Lord with all of your heart and are seeking a very close relationship with the almighty God, this verse is vital. If you ask the Holy Spirit to help teach you to pray constantly, to stay in constant communication with the Lord, this kind of constant prayer will become as natural as breathing after a couple of weeks. It takes work, but it's so rewarding!

Here are a few more verses on prayer that I really like:

> Be anxious for nothing, but in everything by prayer and supplication, with thanksgiving, let your requests be made known to God; and the peace of God, which surpasses all understanding, will guard your hearts and minds through Christ Jesus. (Philippians 4:6-7)

> Confess your trespasses to one another, and pray for one another, that you may be healed. The effective, fervent prayer of a righteous man avails much. Elijah was a man with a nature like ours, and he

prayed earnestly that it would not rain; and it did
not rain on the land for three years and six months.
(James 5:16-18)

Are you encouraged yet? I'm so tired of hearing that some
Scripture is only intended for certain people. That is not true!
The Lord hears all the prayers of His saints, not just the prayers
of some.

Now it came to pass in those days that He went out
to the mountain to pray, and continued all night in
prayer to God. (Luke 6:12)

So, how long should we pray? On many occasions, Jesus prayed
for hours. What's wrong with us? Why do we have a hard time
just praying for a half hour or even a few measly minutes?
Before we even start to pray, we must first ask the Holy Spirit
to help us to pray and to concentrate deeply. With His help we
will be able to pray for longer than we ever thought possible.
What a blessing!

I really like this next verse:

LORD, I cry out to You: Make haste to me!
Give ear to my voice when I
Cry out to You.
Let my prayer be set before You as incense,
The lifting up of my hands as the evening sacrifice.
(Psalm 141:1-2)

Wow. When you pray, do you cry out to Him with all your
heart? Are you in such total submission to the Lord that your
prayers are going up as sweet incense to Him? As I have said
before, we are not only supposed to read the Word of God: we
are to live what we read. The Bible is our training manual. We

are to learn to pray as the saints of old have prayed. What a blessing we will receive.

> Then He spoke a parable to them, that men always
> ought to pray and not lose heart. (Luke 18:1)

Do we lose heart when we see that the Lord isn't answering our prayers? First of all, who are we to demand an immediate, intelligible answer? The Lord knows our hearts; He hears us, and He will answer us in His own way. We just have to open up our spiritual eyes and search for the answer. The answer might be down another road, and it might not be the answer we expecting. Be alert; stay in prayer and in the Word.

> For the eyes of the LORD are on the righteous and
> His ears are open to their prayers; But the face of the
> LORD is against those who do evil. (1 Peter 3:12)

Yes, His eyes and ears are on us and we know that He hears our prayers! Praise the Lord! Be careful, make sure that you are righteous, because He is against anyone who does evil and if you are in this category, this might be the reason you are not being heard by the Lord.

> Evening and morning and at noon I will pray,
> and cry aloud and He shall hear my voice. (Psalm
> 55:17)

Chapter 5

What about Worship?

Oh, worship the Lord in the beauty of holiness!
Tremble before Him, all the earth. (Psalm 96:9)

Give unto the LORD, O you mighty ones,
Give unto the LORD glory and strength,
Give unto the LORD the glory due to His name;
Worship the LORD in the beauty of holiness. (Psalm
29:1-2)

First, let's get a handle on the word "worship." What exactly
is worship? Worship is admiration: to be in awe, and to show
love, reverence, devotion, amazement and respect.

Here are a few verses, early in the Bible, that use the word
worship.

And Abraham said to his young men, "Stay here
with the donkey; the lad and I will go yonder and
worship, we will come back to you." (Genesis 22:5)

> Then the man bowed down his head and worshiped the LORD. (Genesis 24:26)

> So He said, No, but as commander of the army of the LORD I have now come, And Joshua fell on his face to the earth and worshiped and said to Him, What does my Lord say to His servant. (Joshua 5:14)

In that passage, Joshua is worshiping the Lord in hopes of hearing an answer from the Lord.

> Now He said to Moses, Come up to the LORD, you and Aaron, Nadab and Abihu, and seventy of the elders of Israel, and worship from afar. (Exodus 24:1)

This verse tells us that the Lord invited Moses, Aaron, his two sons, and seventy elders to worship Him. The Lord wants us to worship Him.

> But if your heart turns away so that you do not hear, and are drawn away, and worship other gods and serve them, I announce to you today that you shall surely perish. (Deuteronomy 30:17-18a)

Worship is so important to our God that if anyone worships another god, that person will perish.

> Then they will answer, Because they forsook the LORD God of their fathers, who brought them out of the land of Egypt, and embraced other gods, and worshiped them and served them; therefore He has brought all this calamity on them. (2 Chronicles 7:22)

This shows us that worship belongs only to our God, and there can be great consequences if we worship other gods.

> Then Job arose, tore his robe, shaved his head; and
> he fell to the ground and worshiped. (Job 1:20)

When Job was going through such great heartache, he would fall down and worship the Lord. We learn everything about worship through Scripture. The Lord teaches us through His word.

All throughout the Psalms, David worships the Lord with all of his heart. We can learn from David how to worship and to please the Lord.

> But as for me, I will come into Your house in the
> multitude of Your mercy; In fear of You I will
> worship toward Your holy temple. (Psalm 5:7)

> All the ends of the world Shall remember and turn
> to the LORD, and all the families of the nations Shall
> worship before You. (Psalm 22:27)

> All the earth shall worship You and sing praises to
> You; They shall sing praises to Your name. (Psalm
> 66:4)

> Lift up your hands in the sanctuary and bless the
> LORD. (Psalm 134:2)

We are also to lift up our hands toward the Lord in worship, to bless the Lord.

> I spread out my hands to You; My soul longs for You
> like a thirsty land. (Psalm 143:6)

Like King David, we are to worship with all our hearts and souls.

> Then David danced before the LORD with all his might; and David was wearing a linen ephod. (2 Samuel 6:14)

> Praise Him with the timbrel and dance; Praise Him with stringed instruments and flutes! (Psalm 150:4)

We, also, are meant to worship the Lord by raising our hands up to Him and dancing. If you would go to a Messianic Jewish Synagogue (Jewish believers in Jesus Christ. In the day of Jesus, they would have been His followers.), and attend their wonderful Saturday morning service, you would see them raising their hands in worship. Also, in the corner of the sanctuary, you would see beautiful organized dancers, just dancing unto the Lord. It's such a heartwarming sight. I highly recommend all strong Christians to attend at least one of their services. They are so on fire for Jesus and could put some Christian churches to shame.

Their entire service is unique. You will hear some Hebrew and English, but the rabbi's message is in English. All are welcome. If you decide to go for the experience, I suggest you arrive ten to fifteen minutes early and plan to be there for a few hours. It is well worth the time. You don't want to miss anything!

Now let us take a look at worship in the New Testament.

Worship is so important that even Satan tries to get Jesus to worship him.

> And he said to Him, "All these things I will give You if You will fall down and worship me." Then Jesus said to him, "Away with you, Satan! For it is written, You shall worship the LORD your God and Him only you shall serve." (Matthew 4:9-10)

> And in vain they worship Me, teaching as doctrines
> the commandments of men. (Matthew 15:9)

We must be very careful not to worship the Lord with lip service. We must follow the commandments of the Lord and not the made-up commandments of man, as we see with this verse:

> But the hour is coming, and now is, when the true worshipers will worship the Father in spirit and truth; for the Father is seeking such to worship Him. God is Spirit, and those who worship Him must worship in spirit and truth. (John 4:23-24)

As the verse says, God is spirit. We must close our eyes, picture the Lord, and shower Him with our worship in spirit. We are not to worship the Lord by simply reading or speaking the words aloud; we are to be truthful. Those words of worship must be heart-filled, and we should mean every word with all our hearts.

> Then the four living creatures said, "Amen!" And the twenty-four elders fell down and worshiped Him who lives forever and ever. (Revelation 5:14)

> ... saying with a loud voice, Fear God and give glory to Him, for the hour of His judgment has come; and worship Him who made heaven and earth, the sea and springs of water. (Revelation 14:7)

So yes, we are to worship the Lord always. The God of Abraham, Isaac, and Jacob; the creator of the heavens, the earth, and everything on and beneath it—we must worship Him. Our Lord is so worthy! Amen and amen.

Chapter 6

Holiness

For I *am* the LORD your God. You shall therefore sanctify yourselves, and you shall be holy; for I *am* holy. (Leviticus 11:44)

The Lord said to "be holy; for I am holy." This is what holiness means to me.

The Word is telling us to be a reflection of God in whatever we do. We should keep striving to get as close to our God as humanly possible. When people see and hear us, they should see the holiness of God in us because of our constant prayer and constant reading of His word. We are to be set apart from everyone else; we are not to be a part of this world or to even see this world through worldly eyes. Instead, we are meant to continuously strive to see the world through the eyes of our Lord. I believe being holy as He is holy means that we are to be in constant union with our almighty God, and He will allow us to be a reflection of Christ through us, and be glorified through everything we do and say.

Constantly striving to be holy is a never-ending process. When people see and watch us, they will see that we are different and they'll always wonder why. The answer is that our God commands us to obey Him and serve our Creator fully, with everything we have. We must always keep on striving to be holy, for He is holy. If we don't, then who are we serving? There isn't any in-between: we are to follow either the Lord or Satan.

> I know your works, that you are neither cold nor hot. I could wish you were cold or hot. So then, because you are lukewarm, and neither cold nor hot, I will vomit you out of My mouth. (Revelation 3:15-16)

The greatest fear I think the saint should have is at the time of judgment. When we are standing in front of the Judgment seat of Christ, what will He say to us?

> But why do you judge your brother? Or why do you show contempt for your brother? For we shall all stand before the judgment seat of Christ. For it is written: "As I live, says the LORD, Every knee shall bow to Me, and every tongue shall confess to God." So then each of us shall give account of himself to God. (Romans 14:10-12)

> For we must all appear before the judgment seat of Christ, that each one may receive the things done in the body, according to what he has done, whether good or bad. (2 Corinthians 5:10)

Will God say to you, "Well done, my faithful servant"? Or will He tell you He does not know you and tell you to depart from Him?

> Then you will begin to say, 'we ate and drank in Your presence and You taught in our streets.' But He

will say, 'I tell you I do not know you, where you are from. Depart from Me, all you workers of iniquity. (Luke 13:26-27)

In Matthew 7 we read further how the Lord will reject those who never knew him:

> Therefore by their fruits you will know them. Not everyone who says to Me, Lord, Lord, shall enter the kingdom of heaven, but he who does the will of My Father in heaven. Many will say to me in that day, Lord, Lord have we not prophesied in Your name, cast out demons in Your name, and done many wonders in Your name? And then I will declare to them, I never knew you; depart from Me, you who practice lawlessness! (Matthew 7:20-23)

The Lord created us to have fellowship with Him. The problem that so many of us have is that our Lord gave us free will. We tend to want to exercise our free will and live for our own selfish needs. Consequently, we turn our backs on our creator, our God. This includes putting ourselves, our spouses, our children, and our money before our God. That is wrong! He gave us our spouses as a gift, for companionship; He gave us our children as a gift to raise for Him, and then to let them go and to serve Him; He gave us our money as a gift to use to serve Him.

> No one can serve two masters; for either he will hate the one and love the other, or else he will be loyal to the one and despise the other. You cannot serve God and Mammon. (Matthew 6:24)

> For the love of money is a root of all kinds of evil, for which some have strayed from the faith in their

greediness, and pierced themselves through with many sorrows. (1 Timothy 6:10)

No one is ever to be placed above our God in our lives. We are not to live our lives for ourselves or anyone else; we live only to serve God. We are to obey Him and be holy, for He is holy.

Chapter 7

Fasting: Why Fast?

I was never told about fasting while growing up in the church. If it's not that important, then why fast? No one else does.

For some reason in this day and age, fasting is not discussed, and it really should be. Fasting is present throughout Scripture—in both Old and New Testaments.

> My knees are weak through fasting, And my flesh is feeble from lack of fatness. (Psalm 109:24)

> Now the king went to his palace and spent the night fasting. (Daniel 6:18)

> Then I set my face toward the Lord God to make request by prayer and supplications, with fasting, sackcloth and ashes. (Daniel 9:3)

> "Now, therefore," says the LORD, "Turn to Me with all your heart. With fasting, with weeping and with mourning." (Joel 2:12)

"Moreover, when you fast, do not be like the hypocrites, with a sad countenance. For they disfigure their faces that they may appear to men to be fasting. Assuredly, I say to you, they have their reward." (Matthew 6:16)

So Cornelius said, "Four days ago I was fasting until this hour; and at the ninth hour I prayed in my house, and behold, a man stood before me in bright clothing." (Acts 10:30)

Do not deprive one another except with consent for a time, that you may give yourselves to fasting and prayer; and come together again so that Satan does not tempt you because of your lack of self-control. (1 Corinthians 7:5).

But in all things we commend ourselves as ministers of God: In much patience, in tribulations, in needs, in distresses, in stripes, in imprisonments, in tumults, in labors, in sleeplessness, in fasting. (2 Corinthians 6:4-5)

So, as you can see, both testaments describe fasting. My suggestion is for you to pray about it and see where the Lord leads you in your quest for a closer relationship with Him while practicing fasting.

We can think of many reasons to not follow the Lord in fasting, such as its difficulty, our pleasure in eating, and that it doesn't fit into our lifestyles. This makes me wonder, is it the Lord who gives you these reasons not to fast, or is it Satan?

Believe me; Satan doesn't want you to fast. He will try very hard to keep you from growing closer to the Lord in any way he can.

Is fasting hard? Yes, it is. I see fasting as bittersweet. It's bitter because it's so hard, and while you fast, you really look forward to it being over. It's sweet because you see the closeness you feel to the Lord: it is totally indescribable. Once it's over, you can't wait until next month to fast again.

When fasting, you can keep up with your everyday life. The Lord expects us to do this. Go to work and be as normal as ever. People don't have to know that you're fasting. Just be yourself. While fasting, always stay in prayer throughout the day (remember, "pray without ceasing"). Be mindful of future plans when planning a fast. When making luncheon plans with associates, for instance, check your calendar to make sure it isn't a fasting day. The Lord comes first.

When fasting more than one day in a row, break up your routine. One night after work, go into your private room to study and pray for the evening. The next night, dedicate the evening to worship; put your worship music on and picture the face of the Lord and spend the evening in wonderful, heart-filled worship. The next evening, stay in deep prayer. Before you know it, the fasting has ended. You will be greatly blessed by the Lord.

There is one caution that I have to mention. If the Lord gives you a few days in a row each month to fast, don't break the fast! This can be a very big mistake. If the Lord gives you a certain number of days to fast and you're unable to keep those days, don't toss aside the fast prematurely. Move the fasting days to another week, when you can dedicate them more fully unto the Lord. He won't honor a broken fast. The Lord comes first.

One other thing about fasting: keep it private.

Many people will tell you that they are fasting right now! They'll go on and on about a decision their church made for their people to fast on this day or that day. They will make sure that everyone they talk to knows that they are fasting.

> Moreover, when you fast, do not be like the hypocrites, with a sad countenance. For they disfigure their faces that they may appear to men to be fasting. Assuredly, I say to you, they have their reward. But you, when you fast, anoint your head and wash your face, so that you do not appear to men to be fasting, but to your Father who is in the secret place; and your Father who sees in secret will reward you openly. (Matthew 6:16-18)

Don't let this be you. Don't decide to fast because someone tells you to do it. You are to fast because you want to become closer to your God through fasting. It's between you and the Lord, not you and your church.

Chapter 8

Faith

What is faith?

You can say that you have faith that the sun will rise every morning.

You can have faith that on a clear night you will see the stars in the sky.

Faith is belief with strong conviction. It's a firm belief in something for which there may be no tangible proof. It's complete trust: the opposite of doubt.

There are different types and levels of faith. Secular faith describes your faith that the sun will rise in the morning and that the stars will be apparent at night. All people share this faith, no matter their religion. They have faith that rain will come in a drought. They don't know when, but they have faith that the rain will come sooner or later.

People that believe in God have faith. They believe in something that they can't see, but by faith they believe that there is a God and that He created all things on the earth, under the earth, and in the heavens. They believe that there is a Holy Spirit according to Scripture, even though they can't see him. They believe that Jesus is the Messiah, the Son of God that was promised in the Old Testament. He was born of a virgin, died a sinner's death, according to Scripture, and was buried in a rich man's tomb. On the third day, he rose again—all according to Scripture. People of faith believe He bore our sins on the cross to wash them away. They believe it all by faith.

> Now faith is the substance of things hoped for, the evidence of things not seen. For by it the elders obtained a good testimony. By faith we understand that the worlds were framed by the word of God, so that the things which are seen were not made of things which are visible. (Hebrews 11:1-3)

Chapter eleven of Hebrews is filled with the faith of the prophets. It would be good for you to read it on your own. I will share one more verse from this chapter that I really like:

> But without faith it is impossible to please Him, for he who comes to God must believe that He is, and that He is a rewarder of those who diligently seek him. (Hebrews 11:6)

This verse describes a different level of faith. The servants believe Hebrews 11:6, and commit their lives to serving the Lord. When someone totally commits his or her life to serving the Lord, this commitment brings him or her to a new place. Sometimes it is on the front lines of the spiritual battlefield. It seems a strong faith is needed most when the Lord brings a saint to uncharted waters, to use the saint in a new place.

It is a very scary time in the servant's life when the Lord leads her to break out of her comfort zone, when He places her on the front lines of the spiritual battlefield. The servant has all the faith that she thinks she needs. She thinks she's armed with the armor of the Lord and ready for whatever comes her way, but she is not. I know someone in this situation. An associate of mine thought she had all the faith that she would ever need and was ready for the new season of service in which the Lord had placed her. Unfortunately, she was wrong. This new season was a learning experience in more ways than one. There was bad spiritual warfare brewing, and there were people that were indwelled by demons and others who were filled with very evil spirits that began attacking the Holy Spirit within my friend.

She had her faith and was very strong in her faith, but what she was experiencing was very foreign to her; she had no idea this kind of spiritual warfare really happened in real life. She was afraid and didn't know what to do. The Lord brought a friend to her that belonged to a church that deals with spiritual warfare. She then had a meeting with the pastor. During the meeting, the pastor asked her a question that was like a dagger going through her heart. He asked her, "Where is your faith?" She was floored. She explained to him that she had more faith than anyone could ever have. He then asked, "If you have so much faith, than why are you talking to me?" She told him it was because she was fearful for her life and didn't know what else to do. He then instructed her to build upon the faith that she had and that the Lord would protect her and He would be glorified.

My friend cried all the way home. How could he say that she didn't have faith? That night, through her tears, she prayed for an overabundance of faith. She did some Scriptural research on faith and found all the Scriptures that she needed to make her faith greater than ever. She made printouts of all the Scriptures, memorized them, and kept them with her always. She was then ready for the season. She was a new person, servant, and warrior for the Lord. She was no longer scared about being attacked, mugged, or fearful of her life. The Lord was in total control and in charge. She was well protected and full of confidence and *faith*.

This season of servitude lasted a few years, and the Lord used her greatly in His service. She learned so much, and all her experiences were priceless. The Lord led her and guided her every step of the way. It was a spectacular season, and the Lord was highly glorified through it all.

> But the Lord is faithful, who will establish you and guard you from the evil one. (2 Thessalonians 3:3)

Praise the Lord!

Chapter 9

Spiritual Warfare

When we are used for the Lord, Satan starts to pay particular attention to us. You are a real threat to Satan, so you may start to experience spiritual warfare. Spiritual warfare consists of evil demons and spirits fighting the Holy Spirit that's within you. It can be very scary, and you must learn as much as you can about how to be a true warrior for our Lord to combat the spiritual warfare. Read and learn as much as possible. The Lord must be glorified through your new season on the front lines of the battlefield. The more of a threat you are to Satan, the stronger his attacks will be toward you. Be prepared and keep building on your faith! The Lord must be glorified!

If you see warfare going on in your church as well as your workplace, I highly recommend you to do the following:

Pray every morning before you leave the house: go into your private place and pray for at least a half hour, then read the word of the Lord for another half hour. While in prayer, ask the Lord to prepare and to protect you for the day's upcoming battle. Pray that the Lord will place a wall of protection around you that Satan, his evil spirits, and demons will not be able to penetrate. They will be placed under your feet this entire day in the name of Jesus. Pray that the Lord will use you as a tool this very day. Ask that He will bless you and use you on the front lines of the battlefield to bring Him full honor and glory. Pray for strength, courage, wisdom, faith, and boldness to be the warrior that would please the Lord.

Don't let Satan's worldliness pull you down! He will try. Always remember, we are not pleasing the Lord by backing down because of lack of faith. We would then be pleasing to Satan! That can't happen! We cannot give Satan any glory. He will try very hard to give us a hard time so we will stop being a witness for the Lord! We must be strong in the Lord and keep on "praying without ceasing" for the strength and faith that we need to go on. When he knocks us down, we must get right back up again and continue to be a strong warrior for our Lord!

All of the glory belongs to the Lord. Also, you must not forget the Spiritual Warfare Prayer. You must protect yourself every morning.

The following is a great prayer that has and still does help me greatly through my times on the front lines of the battlefield. Use it as an example and a guide for when you pray for protection. If you forget to say the prayer one morning, you will see a big difference! You won't be fully protected. Satan will sneak in the back door and you will be hit hard that day on the battlefield. A friend of mine gave me this "Spiritual Warfare Prayer" many years ago, it touches all the bases.

Spiritual Warfare Prayer

Heavenly Father, I pray this prayer in the power of the Holy Spirit and in the name of Your Son Jesus Christ, who shed His blood to redeem us from the curse of the law and to save us from death, hell, and the grave.

I claim (Matthew 16:19), that we have the keys to the Kingdom of heaven, which gives us the Authority to bind and to loose. That whatever we bind on earth is bound in heaven and whatever we loose on earth is loosed in heaven.

I bind, Rebuke and bring to no effect:
All division, discord and disunity . . .
All rebellion, disobedience, confusion, and disorder . . .
All strife, anger, wrath, murder, hatred, and violence . . .
All criticism, condemnation, vain glory, envy, jealousy, and gossip . . .
All slander, evil speaking, and filthy communication out of any mouth . . .
All lying, hindering spirits . . .
All retaliatory spirits . . .
All deceiving and scorning spirits . . .
All false teachings, false gifts, manifestations, all lying signs and wonders . . .
All poverty, lack or want, and fear of lack . . .
All murmuring and complaining spirits, all seducing spirits, all spirits of the Antichrist, all occult and witchcraft spirits . . .
All spirits of false witness and fault-finding . . .
I break all curses that have been placed on us . . .
I break the power of negative words and attitudes coming out of the mouths of people.
I break all generational curses and diseases.
I come against all strongholds that bind up the people.
I break and render useless all prayers not inspired by the Holy Spirit—whether psychic, soul force, witchcraft, or counterfeit tongues—that have been placed against me.
I am free from all demonic forces, and whom the Son sets free is free indeed!
I submit myself to God. I will resist the Devil and he must flee.
For no weapon formed against me shall prosper, and every tongue that speaks against me, you shall condemn.

I put on the whole armor of God.

Your Word says that the steps of a good man are ordered by the Lord.

The Holy Spirit guides me into all truth. I discern between the righteous and the wicked, between those that serve God and those that do not.

I take authority over this day in the name of Jesus. Let it be prosperous for me, let me walk in your love with compassion for my fellow man and show forth your glory in the earth. I take authority over Satan and all of his demons and those people that are influenced by them. I declare that the Devil is under my feet and shall remain there throughout this day.

I plead the blood of Jesus over every area of my life and that of my family's lives. I claim household salvation.

I declare unity in our church by Christ Jesus; I close the door that was open to give legal right to any spirit or demon . . .

And I loose the Spirit of God to overcome every evil force.

In Jesus' name I pray, Amen.

Every morning in the workplace, anoint each doorway with the blood of Christ: place your hands on both sides of the doorframe and say, "blood of Christ." Do this with all the doorframes throughout your work.

Also, every morning, get rid of the evil spirits by chasing them away. Say, with authority, "Satan! If you or if any of your evil spirits or demons are in this place, I demand you, in the name of Jesus Christ, to flee from here and go into outer darkness; for you're not welcome here! The Holy Spirit of God fills this entire place—every office and every room."

Then pray for the Holy Spirit to fill the entire room. You need to cast the evil spirits into "outer darkness" because they need a place to go or they will return.

During my spiritual warfare, I would do this routine every morning. You need the protection.

At church, if you are holding a conference or a revival, Satan and his evil spirits will be there unless the sanctuary is protected. Do the same as above with the blessings and anointing. Also, anoint each pew with the blood of Christ.

If the spiritual warfare is really bad in the workplace, or wherever you are being used, be careful! Satan can follow you home and start attacking you there! Do the same anointing throughout your entire house daily!

Here are a few verses that have always helped me when I was going through some really bad spiritual warfare:

> Fear not, for I am with you: Be not dismayed, for I am your God. I will strengthen you, Yes, I will help you, I will uphold you with My righteous right hand. (Isaiah 41:10)

> Have I not commanded you? Be strong and of good courage; do not be afraid, nor be dismayed. For the LORD your God is with you wherever you go. (Joshua 1:9)

> The eternal God is your refuge, and underneath are the everlasting arms; He will thrust out the enemy from before you, and will say, Destroy! (Deuteronomy 33:27)

> Yea, though I walk through the valley of the shadow of death. I will fear no evil: For You are with me: Your rod and Your staff, they comfort me. (Psalm 23:4)

> For God has not given us a spirit of fear, but of power and of love and of a sound mind. (2 Timothy 1:7)

> Now the just shall live by faith; but if anyone draws back. My soul has no pleasure in him. (Hebrews 10:38)

Hebrews 10:38 is a big deal to me. I'm here to serve the Lord, so this verse keeps me building my faith. I don't want to fall back. I don't want the Lord to be unhappy with my service to Him. Displeasing the Lord would be like a dagger going through my heart. This verse keeps me strong to overcome any and all spiritual warfare. My life is to please the Lord, to be used by Him for His honor and glory, not for me to fall back and for Him not have any pleasure in me. I pray that you feel the same way. Praise the Lord for His written word and for the constant encouragement He gives us through Scripture.

Recall the information in the previous chapter regarding the consequences of turning back and refusing the Lord. This includes telling Him that you don't want to be around spiritual warfare for whatever reason. *There will be consequences for us to face if we refuse to let the Lord use us where He has placed us.* We must break through our comfort zone and go down the road that the Lord has prepared for us. We can and must learn from the experiences that He wants us to go through. Just be careful!

Chapter 10

Is it Backsliding?

So, you are a servant of our Lord. He uses you greatly in the workplace; He keeps on bringing you in and out of different seasons of service to Him. He has been using you for the past couple of years with unbelievers, and the Lord is glorified by your service. Well, praise the Lord! That's great!

Now, as time goes on, the Lord stops bringing people to you. You think it's strange that you're being left alone now. You may also be happy for the break.

Now, step back. Look at the situation. Go through your days and see if there is something going on here. I know you're comfortable: you're at ease, the stress of serving the Lord at work is gone for a while. Now you just have one job in the workplace, and you can relax during your breaks and during your lunch hours. You're able to go right home after work, and you don't have to do any research for the next day's witnessing. Yes, this is good: a reprieve!

Are you looking at your days yet? Is everything the same from morning until night? Did the Lord really give you a vacation from serving Him? Let's look at the big picture:

Do you wake up in the morning and still pray for at least a half hour and still have a half hour in the Word of God? At night, do you still pray for at least a half hour? Do you read the Word or study the Scriptures at all in the evening? My guess is no.

If you no longer do the above, then my guess is that you have backslidden. Let's get you back into your old routine of studying the Word and spending time deep in prayer. Don't give Satan the glory of your enjoyment of time to yourself. You must serve the Lord.

No, the Lord doesn't give us a vacation from serving Him, and we shouldn't want one! Don't be fooled by Satan when he uses our fast-paced lives with our jobs and families to keep us from serving the Lord. We have a race to run with all of our might; get back on the racetrack and the prize will be outstanding!

We have to be really careful not to take our eyes from the Lord. Satan will try very hard to distract us with our family and friends and by leading us to become complacent with serving the Lord. If we end up praying for five minutes a day, or we're so involved with the kids that we put off studying the Word, Satan will be in his glory. We can't let that happen.

> Do you not know that those who run in a race all run, but one receives the prize? Run in such a way that you may obtain it. And everyone who competes for the prize is temperate in all things. Now they do it to obtain a perishable crown, but we for an imperishable crown. (1 Corinthians 9:24-25)

Chapter 11

I Just Can't Stop Worrying

I know I'm saved and I love the Lord with all my heart. I just have so much going on in my life now, and I'm a nervous wreck. I have talked to my pastor so many times that he won't see me anymore, my friends are so tired of hearing me complain that they avoid me, and my family members tune me out. I'm going crazy! I need to talk, I need to vent, and now everyone is staying away from me. I'm making mistakes at work because I'm unable to concentrate on my job. I have daily Scripture readings on my desk along with all kinds of encouraging verses, but those don't help my anxiety. Nothing is working!

There are so many people that are going through something like this now. I know it's hard, but stop trying to rely on everyone else to help you. You are being prayed for by your pastor and other friends. All the praying in the world won't help you if you don't give it to the Lord. You have to totally let go of your problems and hand them over to the Lord.

It's like a child that has a favorite toy that broke. The child goes to his father and asks him to fix the toy. The father reaches for the toy, but the child won't let go of it. "No, it's my favorite toy," the child says. The father in turn tells the child that if he doesn't let go of the toy, he will be unable to fix it. Once the child releases the toy into the hands of the father, he is able to fix the toy and the child is happy once again. The same is true with us. We have to place our problems into the hands of our Father. We have to totally let go of them, and then He will give us peace. We need faith in our Lord, not in ourselves.

When we hold onto our problems and don't turn them over to the Lord, we show a lack of faith. We have to be really careful. We should stay in constant prayer, stay in the Word of God a few times a day, fast for a few days with just water and prayer, and stop placing our burdens on everyone that we know.

Satan hears the things that you say, and he feeds on them! He will make you even more miserable, and he will use your problems to draw you away from the Lord! Stay strong; the Lord knows what you're going through. Here are a few favorite verses to keep you going:

> For I the LORD your God, will hold your right hand. Saying to you, "Fear not, I will help you." (Isaiah 41:13)

> Are not two sparrows sold for a copper coin? And not one of them falls to the ground apart from your Father's will. But the very hairs of our head are all numbered. Do not fear therefore; you are of more value than many sparrows. (Matthew 10:29)

> Casting all your care upon Him, for He cares for you. (1 Peter 5:7)

> Come to Me, all you who labor and are heavy laden, and I will give you rest. (Matthew 11:28)

> God is our refuge and strength. A very present help in trouble. (Psalm 46:1)

The Lord understands, so give your problems to Him and no one else! Keep on reading the Word of God daily and keep in constant prayer.

> Trust in the Lord with all your heart, lean not on your own understanding; in all your ways acknowledge Him and He shall direct your paths. (Proverbs 3:5-6)

The Lord has a plan for you. Stop feeling sorry for yourself. Be strong in the Lord and let Him lead and guide you. We must all carry a cross, but always remember: Jesus had it worse!

> Let your conduct be without covetousness; be content with such things as you have. For He Himself has said, "I will never leave you nor forsake you." (Hebrews 13:5)

Chapter 12

Let's Talk about Suicide

It's so sad to hear about the growing rate of suicide with teenagers today. It's in the papers too often that a teenager commits suicide because of harassment from his or her peers.

What do you think about suicide? Is it wrong? Do these kids have the right to end their lives along with all the other people of all ages who find life too hard?

Let's say that you're a teenager who is transferred to another high school in the middle of the school year. You are uncomfortable because you are the "new person" in the class. The cliques have been formed years ago, and now you need to fit in.

Let's say that you have red hair and the teens in the school decide not to accept you on the basis of your hair color. Being the nice person you are, you do what you can to accept the jokes and move on, or you try to fit in by accepting their ridicule. But, unfortunately, the stage has been set. You are not going to be accepted by any of the cliques. The big cliques classified you as the "eight ball;" the smaller ones won't say anything to you for fear that the tougher kids will start attacking them. You feel depressed, embarrassed, and ostracized.

You never did anything wrong; you never did anything to these kids, so why are they all against you? It isn't your fault that you had to move to another city and have to attend this new high school. Your dad was offered another job and your family had to relocate. You loved the school that you had to leave behind. You had friends and never had to put up with people not liking you.

It seems like every day it gets worse. You can't go home and tell your parents about the problem because they don't need to know your problems and they wouldn't understand anyway. You feel like you can't win. You feel worthless and alone and start to think that maybe your life is a mistake.

You've even tried talking to your guidance counselor, but she proves to be no help at all with canned responses such as, "They just have to get used to you. Give it time." Thanks a lot!

So, what do you do now? It's natural to want to be accepted by your peers. We all need to be accepted, and we all need to have friends. This type of situation can and does get so out of hand that it often leads to skipping school, getting into trouble, and even committing suicide.

We wish that teens who are having difficulty in high school could understand that school is just temporary. In a few years they'll be done and starting a new life away from high school. They have to understand that high school isn't their entire life, that there's more. They have a friend who wants to be as close to them as a brother, and He will love them with an awesome, unconditional love. This friend doesn't care about the color of their hair, whether or not they're pretty enough, or if they're too short. This friend will love them so much that He will give

His life for them. This friend will give them a promise, and He'll show them that they aren't alone.

> Be strong and of good courage, do not fear nor be afraid of them; for the LORD your God, He is the One who goes with you. He will not leave you nor forsake you. (Deuteronomy 31:6)

> And do not fear those who kill the body but cannot kill the soul. But rather fear Him who is able to destroy both soul and body in hell. Are not two sparrows sold for a copper coin? And not one of them falls to the ground apart from your Father's will. But the very hairs of your head are all numbered. Do not fear therefore; you are of more value than many sparrows. (Matthew 10:28-31)

God can show us that we're not worthless, and He'll show his almighty plan to each one of us.

> For I know the thoughts that I think towards you, says the LORD, thoughts of peace and not of evil, to give you a future and a hope. Then you will call upon Me and go and pray to Me, and I will listen to you. And you will seek Me and find Me, when you search for Me with all your heart. (Jeremiah 29:11-13)

This friend wants you to come to Him; He's waiting.

> Come to Me, all you who labor and are heavy laden and I will give you rest. (Matthew 11:28)

> Behold, I stand at the door and knock. If anyone hears My voice and opens the door, I will come into him and dine with him and he with Me. (Revelation 3:20)

> I am the door. If anyone enters by Me, he will be saved and will go in and out and find pasture. The thief does not come except to steel and to kill and to destroy. I have come that they may have life and that they may have it more abundantly. I am the good shepherd. The good shepherd gives His life for the sheep. (John 10: 9-11)

The good shepherd is Jesus Christ; He wants to be your friend forever.

> My sheep hear My voice and I know them and they follow Me. And I give them eternal life and they shall never perish, neither shall anyone snatch them out of My hand. My Father who has given them to Me, is greater than all and no one is able to snatch them out of My Father's hand. I and My Father are one. (John 10:27-30)

He loves you more than anyone ever could; you have to put your whole trust in Him even though you don't understand:

> Trust in the Lord with all your heart and lean not on your own understanding. In all your ways acknowledge Him and He shall direct your paths. (Proverbs 3:5-6)

When you accept your new friend, you will be changed. You won't care about being accepted by anyone else ever again because you will belong to the Lord!

> Therefore, if anyone is in Christ, he is a new creation; old things have passed away; behold all things have become new. (2 Corinthians 5:17)

I tell you the truth, no one can see the kingdom of God unless he is born again. (John 3:3)

For God so loved the world that He gave His only begotten Son, that whoever believes in Him should not perish but have everlasting life. (John 3:16)

Yes, if you accept Jesus Christ as your savior, you will have an inheritance; you will have eternal life, and your citizenship will be in heaven.

For our citizenship is in heaven, from which we also eagerly wait for the Savior, the Lord Jesus Christ. (Philippians 3:20)

That whoever believes in Him should not perish but have eternal life. (John 3:15)

He who believes in the Son has everlasting life; and he who does not believe the Son shall not see life, but the wrath of God abides on him. (John 3:36)

If you will accept Jesus Christ as your best friend, He will give you a wonderful gift of the Holy Spirit.

Do you not know that your body is the temple of the Holy Spirit who is in you, whom you have from God and you are not your own? For you were bought at a price, therefore glorify God in your body and in your spirit, which are God's. (1 Corinthians 6:19-20)

The evil that is filling the high schools comes from Satan. In the next verse, Jesus is talking to the people that are sinful, just like the people who bully in high school:

> You are of your father the devil and the desires of
> your father you want to do. He was a murderer
> from the beginning and does not stand in the truth,
> because there is no truth in him. When he speaks a
> lie, he speaks from his own resources for he is a liar
> and the father of it. (John 8:44)

> For the wages of sin is death, but the gift of God is
> eternal life in Christ Jesus our Lord. (Romans 6:56)

> You shall not murder. (Exodus 20:13)

Suicide is murder, and you are unable to repent from this sin.
God gave us life, so wouldn't you rather give your life to the
Lord?

> For whoever calls on the name of the Lord shall be
> saved. (Romans 10:13)

When you accept Jesus and belong to Him, He is with you
always. You don't have to be afraid of anyone ever again.

> Fear not, for I am with you; Be not dismayed, for
> I am your God. I will strengthen you, Yes, I will
> help you, I will uphold you with My righteous right
> hand. (Isaiah 41:10)

If you're an adult and you see this going on with a niece, nephew,
neighbor, or friend, please help. Don't just assume that they
are okay. Talk to them and befriend them. Tell them about the
Lord Jesus Christ who can love them unconditionally.

Chapter 13

What about Sin?

Knowing Scripture, it is hard to believe that some organized religions don't believe in sin. That's right. Some religions believe that sin does not exist, that we only think it does.

Whoever believes this doesn't know the Holy Bible. Let's look at some of what the Bible tells us about sin:

> O God, You know my foolishness; And my sins are not hidden from You. (Psalm 69:5)

Yes, David knew all about sin.

Let us now see what Isaiah says about sin:

> Wash yourselves, make yourselves clean; Put away evil of your doings from before My eyes, cease to do evil, Learn to do good; Seek justice, Rebuke the oppressor, Defend the fatherless. Plead for the widow. Come now and let us reason together. Says the LORD. Though your sins are like scarlet. They

shall be as white as snow; Though they are red like crimson. They shall be as wool. (Isaiah 1:16-18)

All we like sheep have gone astray; We have turned, every one, to his own way: and the LORD has laid on Him the iniquity of us all. (Isaiah 53:6)

Do you know what the word "iniquity" means? It means sin. The LORD has laid all of our sins upon Jesus, as He was hanging upon the cross for you and for me. Thank you, Jesus!

Create in me a clean heart, O God. And renew a steadfast spirit within me. (Psalm 51:10)

Make my heart clean—clean from what? Oh yes, from sin.

Let's now look at what the New Testament has to say about sin:

The next day John saw Jesus coming toward him, and said, "Behold! The Lamb of God who takes away the sin of the world." (John 1:29)

Now then, we are ambassadors for Christ, as though God were pleading through us; we implore you on Christ's behalf, be reconciled to God. For He made Him who knew no sin to be sin for us, that we might become the righteousness of God in Him. (2 Corinthians 5:20-21)

Whoever commits sin also commits lawlessness and sin is lawlessness. And you know that He was manifested to take away our sins and in Him there is no sin. Whoever abides in Him does not sin, Whoever sins has neither seen Him or known Him. Little children, let no one deceive you. He who practices righteousness is righteous, just as He is righteous. He who sins is of the devil, for the devil has sinned from the beginning. For this purpose the Son of God was manifested that He might destroy the works of the devil. Whoever has been born of God does not sin, for His seed remains in him; and he cannot sin, because he has been born of God. (1 John 3:4-9)

If we confess our sins, He is faithful and just to forgive us our sins and to cleanse us from all unrighteousness. (1 John 1:9)

Did you know that Jesus says that there is one sin that is unforgivable?

Therefore I say to you, every sin and blasphemy will be forgiven men. But the blasphemy against the Spirit will not be forgiven men. Anyone who speaks a word against the Son of Man, it will be forgiven him; but whoever speaks against the Holy Spirit, it will not be forgiven him, either in this age or in the age to come. (Matthew 12:31-32)

Jesus himself said this. Yes, sin is real. Be careful!

Still don't believe in sin? I saved this Scripture for last:

But if we walk in the light as He is in the light, we have fellowship with one another, and the blood of Jesus Christ His Son cleanses us from all sin. If we say that we have no sin, we deceive ourselves, and the truth is not in us. (1 John 1:7-8)

This passage tells us that the blood of Jesus Christ washes us from our sins. So if sin is nonexistent, when why would we need Jesus? Why did Jesus die on the cross? The verse in 1 John says it very well: if we say that we don't have any sin, then we are deceiving ourselves and we are not of God. We are turning our back on God and His Holy Scriptures.

Let us all remember this special verse in the book of Romans:

> For the wages of sin is death, but the gift of God is
> eternal life in Christ Jesus our Lord. (Romans 6:23)

Chapter 14

Some Scriptural Facts

There are many religions that are founded by prophets. You must be very careful and determine if the prophet is from God or from Satan.

Throughout the rest of the book, I'm going to touch on a few organized religions. I'll mention some religions that were started by a prophet and one that was started by Charles Taze Russell, someone who didn't like what the Bible said, so he invented his own religion.

When I refer to "prophet" in the following chapters, I'm also including Charles Taze Russell in this category even though he was not a prophet.

I'm not going to get into detail of the religions; I'm just going to give you an example of a few, what they believe, and what to lookout for.

These religions seem to require that you serve the religion and not the Lord. This is a big red flag. I'm saying this because this type of religion is very strict. It is very organized and controlling, and this religion emphasizes certain biblical verses that relate to the writings of their prophet.

If the writings of the prophet are a contradiction to the Bible, the religious leaders tell their people that the prophet's writings are true and the Bible is wrong or outdated! This message comes from Satan not from God!

> All Scripture is given by inspiration of God and is profitable for doctrine, for reproof, for correction, for instruction in righteousness, that the man of God may be complete, thoroughly equipped for every good work. (2 Timothy 3:16-17)

If the prophet changes Scripture or goes against the Scripture—ignoring what it says, taking away from or adding to it in any way, shape, or form—then that prophet is from Satan.

If that prophet has you reading and studying his own notes more than the Bible, leave immediately.

If these prophets just give you selected verses to know and do not study the entire Bible verse by verse, then they are keeping you from learning the entire Word of God. They are just giving you verses that are compatible to the teachings of the false prophet and not the teachings of God.

If they say that you are unable to get to heaven except through their religion, they don't know Scripture.

> Blessed are the poor in spirit. For theirs is the kingdom of heaven. (Matthew 5:3)

> Rejoice and be exceedingly glad, for great is your reward in heaven, for so they persecuted the prophets who were before you. (Matthew 5:12)

That whoever believes in Him should not perish but have eternal life. (John 3:15)

Then Jesus, looking at him, loved him and said to him. One thing you lack: Go your way, sell whatever you have and give to the poor and you will have treasure in heaven; and come take up the cross and follow Me. (Mark 10:21)

I am the way, the truth and the life. No one comes to the Father except through Me. (John 14:6)

It doesn't say *except through their religion*! It says *except through Me*! That's Jesus Christ talking!

Let not your heart be troubled; you believe in God, believe also in Me. In My Father's house are many mansions, if it were not so I would have told you. I go to prepare a place for you. And if I go and prepare a place for you I will come again and receive you to Myself; that where I am there you may be also. (John 14:1-3)

Every word in the Bible is for all of us! If we belong to the Lord, then He is building a mansion in heaven for us too.

Chapter 15

Home

The word "home" is a very comfortable word: a safe, secure, and protective word. Hearing the word home suggests a place that is yours, a place of residence. There are many different feelings conjured when I think of the word home. Some people have fear, because of a bad home life, which may have been caused by abuse in the home. Some people feel sorrow because of a lost loved one that was always in that home.

Some people are taken away from home against their will, as punishment, because of something that they have done, and they long to return home. There are also some people that are sick or too old and weak to take care of themselves, and they have to be placed in an institution against their will. They all just want to go home.

I decided to include a chapter on home because it is so special. It really hits me while I talk with patients in nursing homes. They all "just want to go home." That touches my heart. I understand, and I try to comfort them as much as I can through Scripture, knowing that they will never see their earthly home again.

It is sad. The ladies remember the kitchen where they always cooked wonderful dinners for their families; they remember the baking of cakes, cookies, and pies that they loved to make. The men remember working in the basement, fixing whatever broke that week, and, oh yes, the ballgames. Going to the baseball, football, basketball, and hockey games! What a thrill that was for them! The smell of the peanuts and doing the wave! It couldn't get any better than that! It's all gone. Now they stay in their wheelchairs all day long and never leave the building. If the nursing home has a courtyard, a loved one might take them for a stroll outside in the summertime. Oh the fresh air; how wonderful! They might see flowers in bloom and enjoy their wonderful aroma along with the sweet, fresh air that the Lord provides. That just might be the highlight of their week.

If they are fortunate, the Lord might bring one of His servants to them to encourage them with what they are going through and open their eyes to Jesus and His promises.

> For our citizenship is in heaven, from which we also eagerly wait for the Savior, the Lord Jesus Christ. Who will transform our lowly body that it may be conformed to His glorious body, according to the working by which He is able even to subdue all things to Himself. (Philippians 3:20-21)

Did you really understand this verse? This is so exciting! Jesus is telling us that our life here on Earth is just temporary because our citizenship is in heaven! After we die, our bodies will be transformed to the same glorious body that Jesus has! How awesome is that? There is a special verse in Revelation that goes very well with this one:

> He who overcomes shall be clothed in white garments, and I will not blot out his name from the

> Book of Life; but I will confess his name before My
> Father and before His angels. (Revelation 3:5)

Did you catch that? We will be clothed in white garments. Have you ever heard of the Book of Life? If you belong to the Lord, your name is in that book. Yes, your name is written in the Book of Life.

Well, I sure think that that is encouraging.

> While we do not look at the things which are seen, but at the things which are not seen. For the things which are seen are temporary, but the things which are not seen are eternal. For we know that if our earthly house, this tent, is destroyed, we have a building from God, a house not made with hands, eternal in the heavens. (2 Corinthians 4:18-5:1)

> That whoever believes in Him should not perish but have eternal life. (John 3:15)

> We are confident, yes well pleased rather to be absent from the body and to be present with the Lord. (2 Corinthians 5:8)

If your church tells you that when your heart stops beating, your spirit will be in limbo or just floating around the earth, they don't know Scripture! Please, leave that religion immediately!

Look at what Paul says: he is torn between staying on earth to serve the Lord and dying to be with Christ.

> For to me, to live is Christ and to die is gain. But if I live on in the flesh, this will mean fruit from my labor; yet what I shall choose I cannot tell. For I am hard-pressed between the two, having a desire

to depart and be with Christ, which is far better. (Philippians 1:23)

These verses are so comforting. The Lord is telling us that when our hearts stop beating, we will be at home with the Lord Jesus Christ. Hallelujah!

The Word of God has so many fantastic verses describing how the Holy Spirit will bring the lost sheep to the Lord.

> For everyone who asks receives and he who seeks finds and to him who knocks it will be opened. (Luke 11:10)

This verse tells us that if you believe in the Lord Jesus Christ, ask Him to come into your life and He will answer. You must knock on the door with all sincerity, and He will answer. He will come unto you.

> Therefore submit to God. Resist the devil and he will flee from you. Draw near to God and He will draw near to you. (James 4:7-8a)

> Jesus said to him, "I am the way, the truth and the life. No one comes to the Father except through Me." (John 14:6)

> Let your conduct be without covetousness; be content with such things as you have. For He Himself has said, I will never leave you nor forsake you. (Hebrews 13:5)

We must be content with our lives as they are. We must all carry a cross just as Jesus has done. His promise in this verse is that He will never leave us or forsake us. He is with us always in our sleep as well as our waking life; He is always here with us. What great comfort He gives us through Scripture!

> The LORD is near to those who have a broken heart and saves such as have a contrite spirit. (Psalm 34:18)

The Lord knows when you're having a hard time, when you're upset and depressed. In Psalm 34:18, He is letting you know that He is near you. Pray to Him and seek His face.

> Seek the LORD and His strength; Seek His face evermore. (Psalm 105:4)

> When You said, Seek My face, My heart said to You, Your face LORD, I will seek. (Psalm 27:8)

The bottom line is that no matter where you are—from the bottom of the deepest sea to the top of the highest mountain—the Lord is always with you and will never leave you. That is a promise from the almighty God. You must do your part and search for the Lord, and cling to the promise that your home is in heaven with the Lord!

Chapter 16

Inheritance

There are so many verses that deal with our inheritance. I would hate for anyone to miss them. I'll share a few with you now for encouragement.

> To open their eyes, in order to turn them from darkness to light, and from the power of Satan to God, that they may receive forgiveness of sins and an inheritance among those who are sanctified by faith in Me. (Acts 26:18)

> To an inheritance incorruptible and undefiled and that does not fade away, reserved in heaven for you, who are kept by the power of God through faith for salvation ready to be revealed in the last time. (1 Peter 1:4-5)

Did you catch where the inheritance is being reserved for you? In heaven—that's where.

> Giving thanks to the Father who has qualified us to
> be partakers of the inheritance of the saints in the
> light. (Colossians 1:12)

Now, that doesn't just mean some of us, like some religions teach. This means all of us are qualified to partake in the inheritance. Teaching this to mean that only some of us have an inheritance is going against Scripture. If you're involved in a religion that excludes you from God's promises, then I would suggest leaving that religion as soon as possible, as they are teaching you false doctrine.

> ... Knowing that from the Lord you will receive the
> reward of the inheritance; for you serve the Lord
> Christ. (Colossians 3:24)

Do you serve the Lord? Colossians 3:24 is for you if you are running the race for the honor and glory of the Lord.

In this next verse from Hebrews, the author tells us the blood of Jesus will cleanse us from dead works to serve the living God.

> And for this reason He is the Mediator of the new
> covenant, by means of death for the redemption
> of the transgressions under the first covenant, that
> those who are called may receive the promise of the
> eternal inheritance. (Hebrews 9:14)

That is you and me. If you are reading this book, He is calling you. Are you going to obey and say, "Yes, Lord, I want to serve you the rest of my life"? Then you will be included in the Lord's inheritance.

The book of Ephesians offers good verses on inheritance as well:

> In Him also we have obtained an inheritance, being predestined according to the purpose of Him who works all things according to the counsel of His will. Ephesians (1:11)

Now, I'm going to share just one verse that tells us who will not have any inheritance from the Lord:

> For this you know, that no fornicator, unclean person, nor covetous man, who is an idolater, has any inheritance in the kingdom of Christ and God. (Ephesians 5:5)

Well, there it is. I hope this encourages you to serve the Lord with all your heart, soul, strength, and might so you can also be included in the Lord's inheritance for His children.

If anyone tells you that you don't have any inheritance in heaven, I hope this information will help you to stand firm on the Word of God, which tells us yes, we do have an inheritance, per Jesus the Christ!

Chapter 17

Eternal

I know what you're wondering. Why in the world is she writing about the word "eternal"? The reason is simple: some people don't understand what the word means. Eternal means everlasting, undying, never-ending, ceaseless, and timeless. "Forever" means everlasting, eternal, ceaseless, without end. The word "everlasting" is mentioned ninety-seven times in the Word of God.

We have in the Word of God, *eternal life, eternal fire and eternal sin.*

I will share a few verses that deal with the word eternal:

> And everyone who has left houses or brothers or sisters or father or mother or wife or children or lands, for My name's sake, shall receive a hundredfold and inherit eternal life. (Matthew 19:29)

Here Jesus is telling Peter that people who leave their homes to serve the Lord (who we call missionaries now) will inherit eternal life. Let's look further.

That whoever believes in Him should not perish but have eternal life. (John 3:15)

Now Jesus is telling us that if we believe in Him, we all will have eternal life. We will live forever with the Lord.

This next verse is a very popular verse; it is known and memorized my many Christians.

For God so loved the world that He gave His only begotten Son. That whoever believes in Him should not perish but have everlasting life. (John 3:16)

In the next verse Jesus is talking with a Samaritan woman. They are at a well and she is drawing up water. He is telling her how she can have everlasting life.

"But whoever drinks of the water that I shall give him will never thirst. But the water that I shall give him will become in him a fountain of water springing up into everlasting life." (John 4:14)

Jesus is referring to spiritual water, not well water, which will quench her thirst for only a short time. Our spiritual water is the Word of God, we must read it, learn it, and live it; and we will have eternal life through Jesus Christ.

In this next verse, Jesus tells us again how to obtain *everlasting life*.

"Most assuredly I say to you, he who hears My word and believes in Him who sent Me has everlasting life, and shall not come into judgment, but has passed from death into life." (John 5:24)

In the verses above, Jesus is speaking to us. If you say that you don't believe in eternal and everlasting life, then, my friend, you are calling Jesus a liar. If your religion teaches such things, leave it immediately!

> All Scripture is given by inspiration of God and is profitable for doctrine for reproof, for correction, for instruction in righteousness, that the man of God may be complete, thoroughly equipped for every good work. (2 Timothy 3:16-17)

This verse tell us that *all* Scripture is given by inspiration of God—not bits and pieces. It is certainly not for us to change the meaning.

Don't believe anyone that tells you that Jesus is incorrect in saying that eternal doesn't mean forever. John 6:47 can't get any clearer:

> "Most assuredly, I say to you, he who believes in Me has everlasting life." (John 6:47)

Do you believe in Jesus? Do you believe Scripture, which tells us that Jesus was born of a virgin, died for your sins, and was raised on the third day? If so, then you have been promised eternal life, which means that your soul will live forever with our Lord.

> "My sheep hear My voice and I know them and they follow Me. And I give them eternal life, and they shall never perish; neither shall anyone snatch them out of My hand."(John 10:27-28)

This verse comforts my soul. Are you the Lord's? Do you follow Him? If so, Jesus is saying that you will have eternal life, and you will never perish. If you are strong and totally focused upon the Lord, then no one will ever snatch you away from Him.

> He who loves his life will lose it and he who hates his life in this world will keep it for eternal life. If anyone serves Me, let him follow Me and where I am, there My servant will be also, if anyone serves Me, him My Father will honor. (John 12:25-26)

This world is temporary; we are to live for eternity. As Jesus promises, if we serve Him we will be where He is forever.

We just spent some time looking at Scripture regarding "eternal life" according to Jesus. Now, let's look at some verses that deal with "eternal fire."

> If your hand causes you to sin, cut it off. It is better for you to enter into life maimed, rather than having two hands, to go to hell, into the fire that shall never be quenched—where Their worm does not die and the fire is not quenched.

> And if your foot causes you to sin, cut it off. It is better for you to enter life lame, rather than having two feet to be cast into hell, into the fire that shall never be quenched—where Their worm does not die and the fire is not quenched. And if your eye causes you to sin, pluck it out. It is better for you to enter the kingdom of God with one eye, rather than having two eyes to be cast into hell fire—where their worm does not die and the fire is not quenched. (Mark 9:43-48)

This is according to Jesus.

What? You say that your religion teaches that hellfire doesn't exist? That's not what Jesus says! Whom do you follow? The prophet or Jesus? I sure hope it's Jesus.

This is what Paul says:

> These shall be punished with everlasting destruction from the presence of the Lord and from the glory of His power. (2 Thessalonians 1:9)

> Please note: This is everlasting destruction and eternal separation from God.

In this next verse, Jesus mentions hellfire as well as *everlasting fire.*

> "Then He will also say to those on the left hand, Depart from Me you cursed, into the everlasting fire prepared for the devil and his angels." (Matthew 25:41)

Yes, according to Jesus Christ, he will separate the people, one from the other. Those on the good side and those who rejected Him on the other side, where they will be cast into "everlasting fire." If your religion tells you that everlasting fire doesn't really mean everlasting, they are calling Jesus a liar. Please leave that religion now!

> "And these will go away into everlasting punishment, but the righteous into eternal life." (Matthew 25:46)

No! Your soul will not die like some religions teach! Matthew 25:46 says "everlasting punishment" not temporary punishment! Read the Scripture for yourself. Don't believe what someone else tells you, as they may be wrong and will steer you in the wrong direction.

Let us not forget the book of Revelation.

> "And the smoke of their torment ascends forever and ever; and they have no rest day or night, who worship the beast and his image and whoever receives the mark of his name." (Revelation 14:11)

> The devil, who deceived them, was cast into the lake of fire and brimstone where the beast and the false prophet are. And they will be tormented day and night forever and ever. (Revelation 20:10)

Well, these are just a few verses to prove my point. I would much rather follow the inspired Word of God than someone who says that "eternal" really just means temporary. Who are we to believe? Jesus or a self-proclaimed prophet?

At the beginning of this chapter I mentioned that there is, eternal life, eternal fire, and eternal sin.

> "Therefore I say to you, every sin and blasphemy will be forgiven men, but the blasphemy against the Spirit will not be forgiven men. Anyone who speaks a word against the Son of Man, it will be forgiven him; but whoever speaks against the Holy Spirit, it will not be forgiven him, either in this age or in the age to come." (Matthew 12:31-32)

> Be very careful how you treat the Holy Spirit. He's here to help, lead, and guide us; we need Him every moment of every day. The almighty God gave Him to us. We will never be forgiven if we blaspheme against Him.

I have heard so many times that God is love, (which is correct). He is only love and will never hurt the people that He has created. They refuse to believe that a loving God would put anyone in such a place as eternal fire.

Let me tell you something: Our God is a jealous God.

> You shall not bow down to them nor serve them. For I the Lord your God, am a jealous God visiting the iniquity of the fathers upon the children to the third and fourth generations of those who hate Me. But showing mercy to thousands, to those who love Me and keep My commandments. (Exodus 20:5)

> For the Lord your God is a consuming fire, a jealous God. (Deuteronomy 4:24)

But you might say no! You just don't believe that God would ever hurt us. He is a loving God, and only love will come from Him.

Consider the story of Noah's ark. Because of all the sin that broke the heart of our God, what did our God do?

> Then the Lord saw that the wickedness of man was great in the earth, and that every intent of the thoughts of his heart was only evil continually. And the Lord was sorry that He had made man on the earth and He was grieved in His heart. So the Lord said, I will destroy man whom I have created from the face of the earth, both man and beast, creeping thing and birds of the air, for I am sorry that I have made them. (Genesis 6:5-7)

> And God said to Noah. "The end of all flesh has come before Me, for the earth is filled with violence

> through them and behold I will destroy them with
> the earth." (Genesis 6:13)

Yes, we have a loving God, but we also have a jealous God, and He will destroy wicked people.

You might say, oh that just happened once and the Lord promised never to do it again. Well, He promised never to flood the earth again. Remember Sodom and Gomorrah?

> For we will destroy this place because the outcry
> against them has grown great before the face of
> the LORD and the LORD has sent us to destroy it.
> (Genesis 19:13)

> Then the LORD rained brimstone and fire on
> Sodom and Gomorrah, from the LORD out of the
> heavens. So He overthrew those cities, all the plain,
> all the inhabitants of the cities, and what grew on
> the ground. (Genesis 19:24-25)

> Then he looked toward Sodom and Gomorrah and
> toward all the land of the plain; and he saw, and
> behold, the smoke of the land which went up like
> the smoke of a furnace. (Genesis 19:28)

So, there are some religious leaders that will tell you:

o God is good and loving and will never hurt the people He created.
o The words "eternal" and "everlasting" really don't mean forever; they just mean temporary.
o There isn't really eternal fire, it's only for a short time, and the fire will go out.

I hope through the Scriptures that I listed you will see for yourself what is true and what is false. I encourage you to read all of the Scriptures and pray for full understanding. I also encourage you to live your life and your service to the Lord according to Scripture and not according to the teachings of a religion.

Chapter 18

Do You Serve Your Church or Do You Serve the Lord?

Organized religion. Is it good? Is it scriptural?

Watch out for religions that claim to follow the Bible but put their own writings and traditions before the Word of God. This occurs when a congregation's leaders interpret the Bible for them, and the congregation only reads selected Scriptures. No doubt some members may be left with a feeling that there's something missing.

There is a danger of serving your religion and not serving the Lord. In these congregations, members are practically forbidden to question the authority of the religion. Members are not to have their own understanding of the verses and are required to accept what the organized religion tells them. Congregations follow what their religion says because they are led to believe that their religion is the only way they can please God and get to heaven. This is against Scripture. If you're involved in this type of religion, leave immediately and never go back!

Christian Churches

I recently had a brother in Christ approach me and ask me what religion I was. I just looked at him and said, "I serve the Lord Jesus Christ, not a religion." It doesn't matter what church I go to—be it an Evangelical, Baptist, or Charismatic. It doesn't matter. The only thing that matters is whom I serve.

There are some people who put down other Christian churches. Let me ask you, if other Christian churches are accepted by Jesus, if Jesus accepts and is glorified by their worship services, who are we to put them down? They are touching the heart of Jesus. They are glorifying Jesus just as much as our church is. Shame on us for putting down other Christian churches!

> But Jesus said to him, "do not forbid him, for he
> who is not against us is on our side." (Luke 9:50)

When I was studying the Torah with the Jewish people of the Reformed and the Conservative movements; I would always question the false teachings in their study guides (the Talmud, the Midrush, or the writings of respected rabbis). I always had Scripture to counter the false teachings. The rabbis always backed down, and most of the time they were just lost for words. They themselves are unaware of all the Scripture in the Hebrew Bible. They just know the lessons that they teach and live by in addition to selected Scripture. These people don't know what the entire Bible has to say. They have only learned particular verses that pertain to the practices of their religion.

The organized religion wants its congregation to stay ignorant because if the people did read the Bible on their own, they would see the great errors of the teachings of their religion. Thus, certain religions only share certain verses with their congregations. Then they pass out their own study guides written by their leaders explaining the passages (out of context), which conform to their religion and or tradition, and not to God. Organized religions can and do tell its people whatever they want to, and the people believe what they are told and are consequently following false doctrine. If you are in this type of religion, leave it immediately!

> All Scripture is given by inspiration of God, and is profitable for doctrine, for reproof, for correction, for instruction in righteousness. That the man of God may be complete, thoroughly equipped for every good work. (2 Timothy 3:16-17)

We are not to follow any organized religion as they can lead the people astray.

If you are a young Christian, don't try to help someone out of this type of religion. Satan will see your weakness and pull you in. I have seen this happen to some pastors. You must be very careful! Continue going to your church to be encouraged, and learn to be equipped for service to the Lord.

> Jesus answered, "I am the way and the truth and the life; No one comes to the Father except through Me." (John 14:6)

See this verse? No one comes to the Father except through *Me*. It doesn't say through a church!

Chapter 19

Baptism

There are organized religions that follow the practice of baptism, not according to the word of God, but according to their own false doctrine. Be very careful. We are to follow the footsteps of Jesus and only Jesus.

> Now when the days of her purification according
> to the law of Moses were completed, they brought
> Him to Jerusalem to present Him to the Lord.
> (Luke 2:22)

This is when they dedicated Jesus to the God. In Christian churches, we dedicate our newborn children to the Lord, and then when the child is of age and wants to live his life for the Lord, he is then baptized as a public testimony of his love for the Lord. Here we see that Jesus was baptized when he was thirty years old, and then He began His ministry.

> When all the people were baptized, it came to pass
> that Jesus also was baptized; and while He prayed,
> the heaven was opened. (Luke 3:21)

> Now Jesus Himself began His ministry at about thirty years of age, being the son of Joseph. (Luke 3:23)

Jesus was not a baby when he was baptized; he was thirty years old, and then he started his ministry. John the Baptist didn't teach him lessons about church doctrine in order to baptize him! John the Baptist didn't tell Jesus that in order to be baptized He had to join his church and follow the rules of His church.

> Scripture tells us, "Then Jesus came from Galilee to John at the Jordan to be baptized by him" (Matthew 3:13).

> When He had been baptized, Jesus came up immediately from the water; and behold, the heavens were opened to Him, and He saw the Spirit of God descending like a dove and alighting upon Him. (Matthew 3:16)

> Then Jesus was led up by the Spirit into the wilderness to be tempted by the devil. (Matthew 4:1)

Please take note: Jesus left John the Baptist and didn't see him again.

This is so important!

You don't have to join a church in order to be baptized. You don't have to follow a church's doctrine in order to be baptized! Baptism is between you and the Lord only! If you want to join the church, it's okay. I'm just telling you that there are organized churches out there that won't baptize anyone unless they join their church and follow their strict doctrine. That is unscriptural!

And again, what restrictions did Philip give to the eunuch before he baptized him?

> Now as they went down the road, they came to some water and the eunuch said, "See, here is water. What hinders me from being baptized?" Then Philip said, "If you believe with all your heart, you may." And he answered and said, "I believe that Jesus Christ is the Son of God." So he commanded the chariot to stand still. And both Philip and the eunuch went down into the water and he baptized him. Now when they came up out of the water, the Spirit of the Lord caught Philip away, so that the eunuch saw him no more, and he went on his way rejoicing. (Acts 8:36-39)

The eunuch never saw Philip again! The only thing the eunuch needed to believe was that Jesus Christ is the Son of God. That's it! Not a whole series of organized church doctrine that comes with church membership. Be careful: anything other than this is unscriptural.

I'm not going to leave out Acts 10.

> There was a certain man in Caesarea called Cornelius, a centurion of what was called the Italian Regiment. A devout man and one who feared God with all his household, who gave alms generously to the people, and prayed to God always. About the ninth hour of the day we saw clearly in a vision an angel of God coming in and saying to him, Cornelius! When he observed him, he was afraid, and said, What is it lord? So he said to him, Your prayers and your alms have come up for a memorial before God. Now send men to Joppa and send for Simon whose surname is Peter. (Acts 10:1-5)

In the following verses, the Lord gives Peter a vision not to call anything unclean which He has made clean. This tells Peter that he should go with the gentiles and tell them about the Lord. So, Peter went with the messengers that Cornelius had sent. After Peter told the crowd about Jesus, this is what happened:

> "Can anyone forbid water, that these should not be baptized who have received the Holy Spirit just as we have?" And he commanded them to be baptized in the name of the Lord then they asked him to stay a few days. (Acts 10:47-48)

Yes, they baptized all of them (please read the entire chapter for yourself). After they were all baptized, they asked Peter and his friends to stay with them for a few days. Then Peter and his friends left and went to their own town. Please note: they were not asked to join their church and follow their doctrine in order to be baptized.

I just want to make one more point. Nowhere in Scripture will you ever see the act of baptizing the dead. Look at this verse in regard to when someone dies:

> Then another of His disciples said to Him, Lord, let me first go and bury my father. But Jesus said to him, "Follow me and let the dead bury their own dead." (Matthew 8:21-22)

There are some religions that baptize the dead, so that the departed will go to heaven. That is not scriptural!

I understand that baptism doesn't have anything to do with salvation. The reason I am mentioning it is because if an organized religion changes one bit of Scripture, if they twist the meaning of just one word like "everlasting," then they won't stop there! If they teach one error than there are many, many more false teachings coming from that church. Be careful. The moment you see the smallest bit of Scripture twisted, use your common sense and leave that church immediately.

We must follow the Word of God, and not man's traditions. Man's traditions will not get us into heaven.

Chapter 20

A Visit to Another Type of Church

The Lord led me to visit another type of church. A gentleman I met there told me that Jesus was behind the curtain on the altar. I asked him who told him that. He then showed me in his church booklet that his statement was true. I in turn told him that what he just showed me was not biblical, that he would not find that anywhere in the written Word of God, the Bible. The church booklet had printed the words of man, not of God.

I asked him if he had ever read the Bible. His reply was no, that his religion didn't require it. The priests tell them what they need to know.

Now this keeps them reliant upon the church, out of fellowship, and far from the Lord. The church has control of them instead of the Lord. The only intercessor we are to have according to Scripture is Jesus.

This gentleman believes in the Lord Jesus Christ and His birth, sacrifice, and resurrection. He tries to be a pillar in his church.

But the sad part is that his organized religion is keeping him from growing in the Lord, from developing a close relationship with the Lord, all because of the traditions of the organized religion. This is one of the reasons Jesus came: to get the Jews to turn away from organized religion, from the traditions of the church, and bring them back to God.

Then the Pharisees and the scribes asked Him, Why do Your disciples not walk according to the tradition of the elders, but eat bread with unwashed hands? He answered and said to them. "Well did Isaiah prophesy of you hypocrites, as it is written:

> This people honors Me with their lips,
> But their heart is far from Me.
> And in vain they worship me,
> Teaching as doctrines the commandments of men.
> For laying aside the commandment of God, you hold
> the tradition of men, the washing of pitchers and
> cups and many other such things you do. He said
> to them, All too well you reject the commandment
> of God that you may keep your tradition." (Mark
> 7:5-9)

The Lord brought another gentleman to me a few days later from the same religion. He was still living in the world. I asked him if he knew for sure that he was going to heaven. He said yes, that he knew he would be going to heaven. I asked him why he believed it, and he responded that he was a good person. I told him that I have known atheists that would give you the shirt off of their backs. Will they be in heaven because they, too, are good people?

The answer is no. These verses explain it very well:

> "Not everyone who says to Me, Lord, Lord, shall enter the kingdom of heaven, but he who does the will of My Father in heaven." (Matthew 7:21)

I asked him if he is doing the will of the Lord in his life and if he has repented of his sins. He said he repents every day, but he had no idea that repentance means to never return to the sin again and to be a new man in Christ Jesus.

> Therefore, if anyone is in Christ, he is a new creation; old things have passed away; behold all things have become new. (2 Corinthians 5:17)

I then asked if he had a Bible. He said that someone gave him one many years ago and admitted that he had no idea what the Bible said. He is a Roman Catholic and told me that his religion doesn't tell them that they have to read the Bible, so he doesn't.

We had a very good, long talk, and he told me that he knew that the Lord brought him to me that day. I then left him in the hands of the Lord.

Any church that tells you that you don't have to read the Bible because they will tell you what you need to know is wrong, and they're keeping you from obtaining a very special, close relationship with Jesus.

By reading the Word of God daily, we learn what the Lord wants us to know. We learn how to live, what pleases the almighty God. We learn what He expects from us and how we are to live and to serve Him. He wants us to read the Word daily and to study His words—to live what we read so that we can please the almighty God with everything we do and say. We should want to have a close relationship with our great Creator so we can be a daily reflection of the Lord. Don't rely on others to tell you what the Bible says. They can be in error, and then you will be totally lost and apart from God forever.

You must open the manual—the Holy Bible—and study it until you know it completely. Then live what the Holy Spirit has taught you. You should make sure that you don't miss a thing! It's good to attend a good Bible preaching church; I suggest a good Baptist church. Learn from the weekly messages, take notes, highlight passages that are important, and study daily the entire Bible, chapter by chapter. The Lord gave us a Bible that a child can understand. Before you even open the book, ask the Holy Spirit to help you to have a full understanding of what you're about to read. I would suggest a couple different versions: the NKJV (New King James Version) this one is an easy-to-read King James Version without the Old English. I would also recommend the NIV (New International Version).

Chapter 21

What Do You Know about our Almighty God?

The Hebrew Bible uses many terms to refer to God. The most explicit name of God is made up of four letters. According to the Jewish tradition, this combination of letters should not be pronounced aloud, for the name of God must be treated with great respect. When this four-letter name appears in the Bible, the Jewish practice is to pronounce it as Adonai, derived from the Hebrew word "Lord."

Other names used in the Bible refer to God is El and Elohim. These terms mean God and are sometimes used to refer to foreign gods as well as the God of Israel. When Elohim refers to foreign gods it is plural. When it refers to the God of Israel, it is singular.

When I took a biblical Hebrew class, the teacher was a highly respected Orthodox rabbi. He was very wise and has been teaching biblical Hebrew for many, many years. When he started teaching us about the names of G d (this is how they would spell it. Out of respect, they always drop a vowel.), he commented that the name "Jehovah" is not in the Hebrew Bible. His words were, and I quote, "Those Jehovah's Witnesses don't know the Bible!"

We compared the translation, and of course he was right. You will not find the name "Jehovah" in the Hebrew Bible. I have no idea why certain versions of the Bible incorrectly translated the name, but it is wrong.

There are so many different religions out there that don't follow the written Word of God. They make up their own doctrine, trying to play God. I have visited and done research on a few of them, and the ones that I refer to follow false prophets and the writings and traditions of man, both of which are against the Bible.

We have such an almighty God. When I look at everything that He has created, everything from the sky, the beautiful trees, the green grass in the fields, the beautiful rainbows, flowers and the sweet aroma that they give, I stand in awe. His creation is nothing short of genius. The chain reaction of all of the insects and animals that help keep the earth so beautiful and make sure that it is constantly replenished is amazing. Not to mention the great bodies of water that sustain all life—the lives of the different animals that live in the oceans and lakes, along with the great pleasures we have enjoying the great bodies of water by swimming, boating, and vacationing on the oceans. He is so worthy of all of our praise and worship!

Let's talk about our almighty God, who exactly is He?

> In the beginning God created the heavens and the earth. The earth was without form, and void; and darkness was on the face of the deep. And the Spirit of God was hovering over the face of the waters.

> Then God said, Let there be light and there was
> light. (Genesis 1:1-3)

If you continue reading through chapters one and two, you will see the LORD creating all things from earth to man, and everything in between.

Where exactly did God come from? So many people would like to know. Since they don't read the Scriptures, they end up making up their own stories that they pass along to anyone who will listen. This in turn leads people down the wrong road and teaches them, according to Scripture, false doctrine.

Some religions teach, according to their prophets, that God spoke to their prophets in person. My question would be, according to Exodus 33:20, with whom did the prophet really have a face-to-face conversation? It surely wasn't God. My guess is just as the Evil One came to Eve in the Garden of Eden, he also went to the false prophets to tell his lies.

> But He said, "you cannot see My face; for no man
> shall see Me and live." (Exodus 33:20)

So this verse tells us that if the prophet says that he had a face-to-face conversation with God, he shouldn't be alive to tell about it. No one has seen God and still live.

> No one has seen God at any time. The only begotten
> Son, who is in the bosom of the Father, He has
> declared Him. (John 1:18)

> "Not that anyone has seen the Father, except He who
> is from God; He has seen the Father." (John 6:46)

God is a spirit:

> "God is Spirit, and those who worship Him must worship in spirit and truth." (John 4:24)

It can't get any plainer than this: God the Father does not have a human form. He is spirit. The next verse tells us what a spirit is:

> "Behold My hands and My feet, that it is I Myself. Handle Me and see, for a spirit does not have flesh and bones as you see I have." (Luke 24:39)

There are religions that say that there are many gods. Let's look into this with Scripture.

> "You are My witnesses," says the LORD, And My servant whom I have chosen,That you may know and believe Me, And understand that I am He. Before Me there was no God formed, Nor shall there be after Me. I even I *am* the LORD. And besides Me there is no savior. I have declared and saved, I have proclaimed, and there was no foreign god among you; Therefore you are My witnesses, says the LORD that I am God. Indeed before the day was, I *am* He. And there is no one who can deliver out of My hand; I work and who will reverse it? (Isaiah 43:10-13)

> Before the mountains were brought forth, or ever You had formed the earth and the world, even from everlasting to everlasting. You are God. (Psalm 90:2)

Just in case you were told that God wasn't in the beginning, this verse tells us that God always was:

> Thus says the LORD, your redeemer. And He who formed you from the womb: I am the LORD, who makes all things. Who stretches out the heavens

all alone. Who spreads abroad the earth by Myself. (Isaiah 44:24)

I am the Lord and there is no other. There is no God besides Me. I will gird you through you have not known Me. That they may know from the rising of the sun to its setting. That there is none besides Me. I *am* the Lord and there is no other; I form the light and create darkness, I make peace and create calamity; I, the LORD, do all these things. Rain down, you heavens from above, And let the skies pour down righteousness; Let the earth open, let them bring forth salvation. And let righteousness spring up together. I, the Lord, have created it. (Isaiah 45:5-8)

Tell and bring forth your case; Yes, let them take counsel together. Who has declared this from ancient time? Who has told it from that time? Have not I, the Lord? And there is no other God besides Me. A just God and a Savior; There is none besides Me. Look to Me, and be saved, all you ends of the earth! For I am God, and there is no other. I have sworn by Myself; the word has gone out of My mouth in righteousness and shall not return. That to Me every knee shall bow. Every tongue shall take an oath. (Isaiah 45:21-23)

The grass withers, the flower fades. But the word of our God stands forever. (Isaiah 40:8)

Please remember, the Word of our God stands forever. It will not become outdated, as there are not any new Scriptures that claim to be more reliable. You don't need any other book to help explain what the Word of God means. It is the Bible and only the Bible. Any other writings from prophets are false. I pray that I have been able to prove this to you through Scripture.

Chapter 22

What Do we Know about Jesus?

Jesus always was:

> In the beginning was the Word, and the Word was
> with God and the Word was *God*. (John 1:1)

This verse is so important. It tells us that the Word, which is
Jesus, always existed. It tells us that the Word, which is Jesus,
is God.

If your Bible changes any word or adds anything in these
verses—if any upper or lowercase letter has been changed—then
you are reading a Bible written by Satan! Throw it out and leave
the religion that wrote that Bible! Stick to the King James Bible
or New King James Bible only.

Be very careful!

New World Translation of the Holy Scriptures is the Bible of
the Jehovah's Witnesses. It is written by the New World Bible
Translation Committee and published by the Watchtower Bible
and Tract Society of New York, Inc. They have made many

errors with their publications. They changed many, many verses to comply with their false teachings!

The New World Translation changed the verse to discredit Jesus. They changed the uppercase "G" in the word "God" to a lowercase "g." They are reducing Jesus to "a god," instead of *the* God that He *is*. The Watchtower places him among many gods, which puts Him on the same level as Satan.

I have only shared one verse with you, but their entire Bible is laced with many other changed verses! Please stay away from this cult!

> "Enter by the narrow gate; for wide is the gate and broad is the way that leads to destruction and there are many who go in by it. Because narrow is the gate and difficult is the way which leads to life and there are few who find it." (Matthew 7:13-14)

Recently I was talking to a colleague at work who is a Jehovah's Witness. I told her that her religion believes that Jesus already returned to earth in the year 1914 and is alive and living in New York. My colleague was unaware of this. The next day she came running over to me and said, "You were right!" She asked her church about it, and they confirmed what I told her. She was so excited.

My response to her was, "I didn't hear about the great headlines of Jesus coming back on that day did you? I didn't hear of the great worldwide rejoicing of the coming of Jesus, did you?"

Of course, all of her answers were no. She then said, "Well, since He came to New York, how was the rest of the world to know?"

Supposedly it was in secret that He came to the main headquarters of her religion, to help run it.

If your religion tells you that Jesus came back already and is alive and well living in New York City, at their headquarters, or anywhere else in the world, this is a lie! Please read the following verse.

> "Then if anyone says to you, Look, here is the Christ! Or There! Do not believe it. For false christs and false prophets will rise and show great signs and wonders to deceive, if possible, even the elect. See, I have told you beforehand. Therefore if they say to you Look, He is in the desert! Do not go out; or Look, He is in the inner rooms! Do not believe it. For as the lightning comes from the east and flashes to the west, so also will the coming of the Son of Man be. (Matthew 24:23-27)

Do you know what this means?

> But Jesus looked at them and said to them, "With men this is impossible, but with God all things are possible." (Matthew 19:26)

Yes, we have an awesome God! With God, all things are possible. I continued telling my colleague just that. When Jesus comes, everyone will see Him, not just a certain group of people in one building. She then said how could everyone see Him around the world at one time? I told her what it says in the Bible: "With God all things are possible." When He comes, everyone around the entire world will see Him at the same time. God has no limitations.

> Behold, He is coming with clouds and every eye will see Him, even they who pierced Him and all the tribes of the earth will morn because of Him. Even so, Amen. "I am the Alpha and the Omega, the Beginning and the End, says the Lord, who is

and who was and who is to come, the Almighty."
(Revelation 1:7-8)

Jesus is not an angel, He is not a god, and He is not a way-shower.

There are some false religions that often use the name of Jesus Christ in the name of their church in an effort to appear Christian. When members of these religions talk to regular people, they frequently try to sound authentic by referring to Jesus and saying some good things about him. However, they are not talking about the true Jesus Christ of the Bible. Be very careful!

> For if he who comes preaches another Jesus whom we have not preached, or if you receive a different spirit which you have not received, or a different gospel which you have not accepted-you may well put up with it! (2 Corinthians 11:4)

> I marvel that you are turning away so soon from Him who called you in the grace of Christ, to a different gospel, which is not another; but there are some who trouble you and want to pervert the gospel of Christ. But even if we, or an angel from heaven, preach any other gospel to you than what we have preached to you, let him be accursed. (Galatians 1:6-8)

The Jesus Christ of the Bible is truly God and Man. So many different churches deny the deity of Christ, refusing to believe that He is God incarnate in the flesh.

- And without controversy great is the mystery of godliness:
- God was manifested in the flesh,

- Justified in the Spirit,
- Seen by angles,
- Preached among the Gentiles,
- Believed on in the world,
- Received up in glory. (1 Timothy 3:16)

If a religion teaches a duality of Jesus Christ, that Jesus is the human man, and that Christ is the divine idea, then that religion is in error.

We are to worship Jesus.

If a religion refuses to worship Jesus Christ, they are in great error.

> Then those who were in the boat came and worshiped Him saying, "Truly You are the Son of God."(Matthew 14:33)

> And as they went to tell His disciples, behold, Jesus met them saying, Rejoice! So they came and held Him by the feet and worshiped Him. (Matthew 28:9)

> But when He again brings the firstborn into the world, He says: "Let all the angels of God worship Him." (Hebrews 1:6)

Clearly, according to Scripture, Jesus is to be worshiped.

The Physical death of Jesus.

There are some religions that don't believe in the physical death of Jesus Christ.

> But when they came to Jesus and saw that He was already dead, they did not break His legs. (John 19:33)

> Pilate marveled that He was already dead; and summoning the centurion, he asked him if He had been dead for some time. (Mark 15:44)

Saying that Jesus didn't have a physical death is going against Scripture. If a religion says Jesus did not physically die, that religion is heretical.

> But God demonstrates His own love toward us, in that while we were still sinners, Christ died for us. Much more than, having now been justified by His blood, we shall be saved from wrath through Him. (Romans 5:8-9)

Jesus was really physically dead when He was placed in the tomb. He was not alive hiding somewhere. He was dead and He did rise again.

> For I delivered to you first of all that which I also received: that Christ died for our sins according to the Scriptures, and that He was buried and that He rose again the third day according to the Scriptures, and that he was seen by Cephas and then by the twelve. After that He was seen by over five hundred brethren at once, of whom the greater part remain to the present, but some have fallen asleep. (1 Corinthians 15:3-6)

Please stay away from religions that have self-proclaimed prophets; you don't know if the prophet has come from God or from Satan! Don't take any chances!

The self-proclaimed prophets have written their own bibles, plus an assortment of other books. Their writings have changed the Word of God badly and have degraded Jesus, the Holy Spirit, along with the Almighty God! Reading their writings would make the saint's skin crawl. These books go against true Scripture.

Anyone that says that the Almighty God has a goddess wife, as Joseph Smith teaches, is heretical.

According to Mormon theology, Jesus is the literal Son of God and the goddess wife. He was born through physical sexual relations with Mary. Joseph Smith taught that the Holy Spirit had no involvement with the birth of Jesus.

> Now the birth of Jesus Christ was as follows: After His mother Mary was betrothed to Joseph, before they came together, she was found with child of the Hold Spirit. But while he thought about these things, behold, an angel of the Lord appeared to him in a dream, saying, "Joseph, son of David, do not be afraid to take to you Mary your wife, for that which is conceived in her is of the Holy Spirit. (Matthew 1:18 and 20)

Mormons also teach that God is married and has a mother and father. This is just one little example of the falsity of their teachings. Please stay away!

Don't just take my word for it. Look into their doctrine yourself! Do your research before attending any church that was formed by a prophet!

I have a hard time with the teachings of the Seventh Day Adventists, a religion that teaches that Jesus is God and that He is also an angel. They believe He is an angel because of this verse:

> For the Lord Himself will descend from heaven with
> a shout, with the voice of an archangel, and with the
> trumpet of God. And the dead in Christ will rise
> first. (1 Thessalonians 4:16)

Did you ever talk on the phone to a woman and think afterward that she had the voice of a man? Does that make the woman a man? Likewise, just because the above verse says Jesus will descend with the voice of an angel, it does not mean that He is an angel.

> But to which of the angels has He ever said: "Sit
> at My right hand, till I make Your enemies Your
> footstool." (Hebrews 1:13)

> For in Him dwells all the fullness of the Godhead
> bodily. (Colossians 2:9)

> Looking for the blessed hope and glorious appearing
> of our great God and savior Jesus Christ. (Titus
> 2:13)

It doesn't read "our great God and savior Jesus Christ, the archangel.

I see the Father calling Jesus God. But I can't find any reference in the KJV of the father calling Jesus an angel. It isn't there. The following verses say it all:

> God, who at various times and in various ways
> spoke in time past to the fathers by the prophets,
> has in these last days spoken to us by His Son, whom
> He has appointed heir of all things, through whom
> also He made the worlds; who being the brightness
> of His glory and the express image of His person,
> and upholding all things by the word of His power,

when He had by Himself purged our sins, sat down
at the right hand of the Majesty on high.

Having become so much better than the angels, as
He has by inheritance obtained a more excellent
name than they.
For to which of the angels did He ever say:
"You are My Son.
Today I have begotten You"?
And again:
"I will be to Him a Father,
And He shall be to Me a
Son"?
But when He again brings the firstborn into the
world, He says:

"Let all the angels of God worship Him."
And of the angels He says: "Who makes His angels
sprits and His ministers a flame of fire." But to the
Son He says:
"Your throne, O God, is forever and ever."(Hebrews
1:1-8 NKJV)

I saw great errors in the Mormon teachings. We all need to
study the Bible, and the Bible alone, without any help from
the self-proclaimed prophets. Self-proclaimed prophets are
human, and all humans make mistakes.

Jesus took away our sins.

The Seventh-day Adventists follow Leviticus 16:10, which reads:

But the goat on which the lot fell to be the scapegoat
shall be presented alive before the LORD, to make
atonement upon it and to let it go as the scapegoat
into the wilderness. (Leviticus 16:10)

They teach that Satan is our scapegoat and that he will bear our sins.

The Blood of our Lord Jesus Christ washes us clean of all sins. If Satan is our scapegoat, then we don't need Jesus. Satan is not to be given *any* credit!

> For the life of the flesh is in the blood and I have given it to you upon the altar to make atonement for your souls; for it is the blood that makes atonement for the soul. (Leviticus 17:11)

> For this is My blood of the new covenant, which is shed for many for the remission of sins. (Matthew 26:28)

> But if we walk in the light as He is in the light, we have fellowship with one another and the blood of Jesus Christ His Son cleanses us from all sin. (1 John 1:7)

> In Him we have redemption through His blood, the forgiveness of sins according to the riches of His grace. (Ephesians 1:7)

> The next day John saw Jesus coming toward him and said, Behold! The Lamb of God who takes away the sin of the world! (John 1:29)

Don't let anyone tell you that Satan is our scapegoat! Jesus and only Jesus can take our sins away. He is the bearer of our sins.

> Who Himself bore our sins in His own body on the tree, that we, having died to sins, might live for righteousness—by whose stripes you were healed. (1 Peter 2:24)

> And from Jesus Christ, the faithful witness, the firstborn from the dead and the ruler over the kings of the earth. To Him who loved us and washed us from our sins in His own blood. (Revelation 1:5)

> For He made Him who knew no sin to be sin for us, that we might become the righteousness of God in Him. (2 Corinthians 5:21)

I would never follow anyone who teaches that the Lord's words are not true. How can you expect to be blessed while following these false teachings?

Prophecies of the Messiah fulfilled in Jesus Christ:

Let's talk a little bit about some prophecies from the Old Testament that Jesus fulfilled. There are many; I'm just going to touch on a few to give you understanding and belief.

Did you know that when Moses was about to die, he told his people that the Lord was going to give them another prophet like himself?

> And the LORD said to me: What they have spoken is good. I will raise up for them a Prophet like you from among their brethren, and will put My words in His mouth, and He shall speak to them all that I command Him. (Deuteronomy 18:17-18)

Then, in the New Testament, Moses' prophecy is fulfilled:

> He first found his own brother Simon, and said to him. "We have found the Messiah" (which is translated, the Christ) (John 1:41)

> Philip found Nathanael and said to him. "We have found Him of whom Moses in the law and also the prophets, wrote—Jesus of Nazareth, the son of Joseph." (John 1:45)

> Nathanael answered and said to Him, Rabbi, You are the Son of God! You are the King of Israel! (John 1:49)

This is just a small sample. You should read the Gospels for yourself. Fall in love with Jesus. Read His words and hang on to all of His promises and His unconditional love.

Malachi also prophesized the coming of the Messiah:

> Behold, I send My messenger, who he will prepare the way before Me. And the Lord, whom you seek. Will suddenly come to His temple, even the Messenger of the covenant. In whom you delight. Behold, He is coming, says the Lord of hosts. (Malachi 3:1)

John the Baptist gives testimony of being the messenger who will prepare the way of the Lord.

> He said; "I am the voice of one crying in the wilderness; Make straight the way of the Lord." As the prophet Isaiah said. It is He who, coming after me, is preferred before me, whose sandal strap I am not worthy to loose. This is He of whom I said, After me comes a Man who is preferred before me, for He was before me. (John 1:23, 27, 30)

In Genesis it is prophesized that the coming Messiah will come from Judah:

> The scepter shall not depart from Judah, nor a lawgiver from between his feet. Until Shiloh comes; and to Him shall be the obedience of the people. (Genesis 49:10)

Then again in the New Testament, the prophecy is fulfilled:

> The book of the genealogy of Jesus Christ, the Son of David, the Son of Abraham: Abraham begot Isaac, Isaac begot Jacob, and Jacob begot Judah and his brothers. (Matthew 1:1-2)

> For it is evident that our Lord arose from Judah . . . (Hebrews 7:14)

Micah prophesized the birth of the Messiah was to be in Bethlehem, and the prophecy was fulfilled in the gospel of Matthew:

> But you, Bethlehem Ephrathah, Though you are little among the thousands of Judah, Yet out of you shall come forth to Me. The One to be Ruler in Israel, Whose goings forth are from of old, From everlasting. (Micah 5:2)

> Now after Jesus was born in Bethlehem of Judea in the days of Herod the king, behold, wise men from the East came to Jerusalem. (Matthew 2:1)

Zechariah prophesized the thirty pieces of silver thrown into the potter's field:

> Then I said to them, If it is agreeable to you, give me my wages; and if not, refrain. So they weighed out for my wages thirty pieces of silver. And the Lord said to me, "Throw it to the potter"—that princely

price they set on me. So I took the thirty pieces of silver and threw them into the house of the Lord for the potter. (Zechariah 11:12-13)

And again in the book of Matthew, the prophecy is fulfilled:

Then Judas, His betrayer, seeing that He had been condemned, was remorseful and brought back the thirty pieces of silver to the chief priests and elders. Saying, I have sinned by betraying innocent blood, and they said, What is that to us? You see to it! Then he threw down the pieces of silver in the temple and departed and went and hanged himself. But the chief priests took the silver pieces and said, It is not lawful to put them into the treasury, because they are the price of blood. And they consulted together and bought with them the potter's field, to bury strangers in Therefore that field has been called the Field of Blood to this day. Then was fulfilled what was spoken by Jeremiah the prophet, thirty pieces of silver, the value of Him who was priced, whom they of the children of Israel priced and gave them for the potter's field, as the Lord directed me. (Matthew 27:3-10)

Zechariah in the Old Testament also prophesizes the triumphant entry into Jerusalem, a prophecy which was again fulfilled in the gospel of Matthew in the New Testament:

Rejoice greatly, O daughter of Zion!
Shout, O daughter of Jerusalem! Behold, your King is coming to you; He is just and having salvation, lowly and riding on a donkey, a colt, the foal of a donkey. (Zechariah 9:9)

Now then they drew near Jerusalem, and came to Bethphage, at the Mount of Olives, then Jesus sent two disciples saying to them. "Go into the village opposite you, and immediately you will find a donkey tied and a colt with her. Loose them and bring them to Me." (Matthew 21:1-2)

So the disciples went and did as Jesus commanded them. They brought the donkey and the colt, laid their clothes on them and set Him on them. And a very great multitude spread their clothes on the road; others cut down branches from the trees and spread them on the road. Then the multitudes who went before and those who followed cried out, saying:

Hosanna to the Son of David!
Blessed is He who comes in
The name of the Lord!
Hosanna in the highest!
And when He had come into Jerusalem, all the city was moved, saying, Who is this? (Matthew 21:6-10)

The book Psalms is jammed full of prophesies of Jesus. I will list a few:

I will open my mouth in a parable; I will utter dark sayings of old. (Psalm 78:2)

That prophecy was fulfilled in Matthew:

All these things, Jesus spoke to the multitude in parables; and without a parable He did not speak to them. (Matthew 13:34)

Psalm 41 also prophesizes Jesus being betrayed by a friend:

> Even my own familiar friend in whom I trusted,
> who ate my bread, Has lifted up his heel against me.
> (Psalm 41:9)

And the gospel of Luke tells us that Judas was that friend:

> And while He was still speaking, behold a multitude;
> and he who was called Judas, one of the twelve, went
> before them and drew near to Jesus to kiss Him. But
> Jesus said to him, "Judas, are you betraying the Son
> of Man with a kiss?" (Luke 22:47-48)

Christ would be hated without a cause:

> Let them not rejoice over me who are wrongfully
> my enemies; Nor let them wink with the eye who
> hate me without a cause. (Psalm 35:19)

> If I had not done among them the works which
> no one else did, they would have no sin; but now
> they have seen and also hated both Me and My
> Father. But this happened that the word might be
> fulfilled which is written in their law, "They hated
> Me without a cause." (John 15:24-25)

None of Christ's bones would be broken:

> He guards all his bones; Not one of them is broken.
> (Psalm 34:20)

> Then the soldiers came and broke the legs of the first
> and of the other who was crucified with Him. But
> then they came to Jesus and saw that He was already
> dead, they did not break His legs. (John 19:32-33)

Psalm 49 also prophesized the resurrection, and evidence of its fulfillment is in the gospels of Mark and Matthew:

> But God will redeem my soul from the power of the grave, for He shall receive me. (Psalm 49:15)

> But he said to them, Do not be alarmed. You seek Jesus of Nazareth, who was crucified. He is risen! He is not here, see the place where they laid Him. (Mark 16:6)

> He is not here; for He is risen, as He said. Come; see the place where the Lord lay. (Matthew 28:6)

The soldiers gambled for his clothes. Yes! This is prophesized in the book of Psalms and fulfilled in Matthew.

> I can count all My bones.
> They look and stare at Me.
> They divide My garments among them, and for My clothing they cast lots. (Psalm 22:17-18)

> Then they crucified Him and divided His garments, casting lots, that it might be fulfilled which was spoken by the prophet: They divided My garments among them, and for My clothing they cast lots. (Matthew 27:35)

Isn't this great! Are you a believer now?

Let me share with you a few other verses of prophecy from the book of Isaiah.

The virgin birth was prophesized in the Old Testament and fulfilled in the gospel of Luke:

Therefore the Lord Himself will give you a sign: Behold, the virgin shall conceive and bear a Son, and shall call His name Immanuel. (Isaiah 7:14)

Now in the sixth month the angel Gabriel was sent by God to a city of Galilee named Nazareth. To a virgin betrothed to a man whose name was Joseph, of the house of David. The virgin's name was Mary. And having come in, the angel said to her, Rejoice, highly favored one, the Lord is with you; blessed are you among women! But when she saw him, she was troubled at his saying and considered what manner of greeting this was. Then the angel said to her. Do not be afraid, Mary, for you have found favor with God. And behold, you will conceive in your womb and bring forth a Son, and shall call His name Jesus. (Luke 1:26-31)

On Christ's silence:

He was oppressed and He was afflicted. Yet He opened not His mouth: He was led as a lamb to the slaughter, and as a sheep before its shearers is silent. So He opened not His mouth. (Isaiah 53:7)

And the chief priests accused Him of many things, but He answered nothing. Then Pilate asked Him again, saying. Do You answer nothing? See how many things they testify against You! But Jesus still answered nothing, so that Pilate marveled. (Mark 15:3-5)

On Christ being numbered with the transgressors:

Therefore I will divide Him a portion with the great, and He shall divide the spoil with the strong, because He poured out His soul unto death, and He was numbered with the transgressors, and He bore the sin of many and made intercession for the transgressors. (Isaiah 53:12)

With Him they also crucified two robbers, one on His right and the other on His left. So the Scripture was fulfilled which says, and He was numbered with the transgressors. (Mark 15:27-28)

It was also prophesized that He was to be buried with the rich:

And they made His grave with the wicked—But with the rich at His death. Because He had done no violence. Nor was any deceit in His mouth. (Isaiah 53:9)

And the prophecy fulfilled in the gospel of Matthew:

Now when evening had come there came a rich man from Arimathea, named Joseph, who himself had also become a disciple of Jesus. This man went to Pilate and asked for the body of Jesus. Then Pilate commanded the body to be given to him. When Joseph had taken the body, he wrapped it in a clean linen cloth. And Laid it in his new tomb which he had hewn out of the rock; and he rolled a large stone against the door of the bomb, and departed. (Matthew 27:57-60)

I listed just a few of the prophecies of Jesus. There are many more throughout the Bible. I recommend reading the Old and New Testaments and doing more research yourself.

Chapter 23

So, What about the Holy Spirit?

Is there really a Holy Spirit of God? Some people would say no, others would say the Holy Spirit is just a divine science or even an active force. Let's go through Scripture to see exactly who the Holy Spirit is. In Genesis we see the first mention of the Holy Spirit.

> The earth was without form, and void; and darkness was on the face of the deep. And the Spirit of God was hovering over the face of the waters. (Genesis 1:2)

Now, the Hebrew Bible, The Tanakh; uses the word "wind" from God.

Now in biblical Hebrew, the word "wind" has the exact Hebrew spelling as the word "spirit". So the New King James Version is correct when using the word "spirit" in Genesis 1:2.

Now according to biblical Hebrew, the spelling of the words spirit, wind, and breath is the same. These words can be used interchangeably throughout Scripture. In the Old Testament, we find the Spirit of God coming upon certain people. I'll give a couple of examples.

> When they came there to the hill, there was a group of prophets to meet him then the Spirit of God came upon him and he prophesied among them. (1 Samuel 10:10)

> And Balaam raised his eyes, and saw Israel encamped according to their tribes; and the Spirit of God came upon him. (Numbers 24:2)

Here God worked through His spirit in Saul's life so that he was able to have the opportunity to exercise a prophetic gift.

> I have heard of you, that the Spirit of God is in you and that light and understanding and excellent wisdom are found in you. (Daniel 5:14)

With this verse we see that not only can the Spirit of God be upon someone, but He can be found in someone too.

Like Daniel, can people see the Spirit of God in you too? That gives us all something to continuously work on. It doesn't stop with Daniel. If we hunger enough, we can have the same Spirit of God within us also.

Again, who is the Holy Spirit?

I think the next verse sums it up in a nutshell. In Acts 5:3-4, it's at a time that people were selling their land and giving the money to the work of the Lord. Ananias and his wife Sapphira also sold some land and promised to give the funds to the Lord's work. But they decided at the last minute to hold back part of the money for themselves.

But Peter said, "Ananias, why has Satan filled your
heart to lie to the Holy Spirit and keep back part of
the price of the land for yourself? While it remained,
was it not your own? And after it was sold, was it not
in your own control? Why have you conceived this
thing in your heart? You have not lied to men but to
God. (Acts 5:3-4)

Satan filled the hearts of Ananias and Sapphira and they
succumbed to the temptations of greed. This verse states that
when they held back the portion of the money, they didn't lie
to the men (who were filled with the Holy Spirit), but they lied
to God. For the Holy Spirit is the spirit of God.

Now the Lord is the Spirit; and where the Spirit of
the Lord is, there is liberty. (2 Corinthians 3:17)

The Holy Spirit is our instructor as indicated in the next few
verses.

However, when He, the Spirit of truth, has come. He
will guide you into all truth; for He will not speak
on His own authority, but whatever He hears He
will speak; and He will tell you things to come. He
will glorify Me, for He will take of what is Mine and
declare it to you. (John 16:13-14)

Yes! The Lord speaks to us today. If not, then this verse
would be in error, and there are not any errors in the holy
Word of God!

There are so many people who believe the Holy Spirit no
longer talks to us, that it just occurs in the Old Testament. This
is so untrue! Throughout the New Testament, the Lord talks
to His people. The reason people don't hear the Lord anymore
is because they don't have the relationship with the Lord that

they need to hear His voice. You have to hunger and keep on striving for that close relationship with the Lord. If you don't, then of course you won't hear anything. Let's look at a few verses on this subject:

> Now an angel of the Lord spoke to Philip, saying, Arise and go toward the south along the road which goes down from Jerusalem to Gaza. This is desert. (Acts 8:26)

As we read on, we see that Philip obeyed and went to the road and saw the Ethiopian. If Philip hadn't had that close relationship with the Lord and didn't obey Him, then the Ethiopian would never have understood what the book of Isaiah was saying about Jesus, and he wouldn't have been baptized by Philip.

If we are servants for our Lord, we must have that close relationship with Him so that He will use us just like he used Philip and the servants in the following verses. Don't miss your opportunity to have that very close relationship with our Lord, to be used by Him like He used the saints before us.

> As he neared Damascus on his journey, suddenly a light shone around him from heaven. Then he fell to the ground and heard a voice saying to him. "Saul, Saul, why are you persecuting Me?" And he said, who are You Lord? Then the Lord said, "I am Jesus, whom you are persecuting. It is hard for you to kick against the goads." (Acts 9:3-5)

It doesn't stop here, let's go on:

> Now there was a certain disciple at Damascus named Ananias; and to him the Lord said in a vision, Ananias. And he said, "Here I am Lord." So the Lord said to him, Arise and go to the street called Straight,

and inquire at the house of Judas for one called Saul of Tarsus, for behold, he is praying. And in a vision he has seen a man named Ananias coming in and putting his hand on him, so that he might receive his sight. Then Ananias answered, "Lord, I have heard from many about this man, how much harm he has done to Your saints in Jerusalem. And here he has authority from the chief priests to bind all who call on You name." But the Lord said to him, "Go, for he is a chosen vessel of Mine to bear My name before Gentiles, kings and the children of Israel. For I will show him how many things he must suffer for My name's sake. (Acts 9:10-16)

We see in these verses that the Lord spoke to Ananias, and that Ananias actually had a conversation with the Lord. Yes! This still happens today! The entire Bible is for all of us, not just bits and pieces, and not just for some people. It is for us all, and that includes you too!

I'm still going to continue on with this thought:

Now, when they had gone through Phrygia and the region of Galatia, they were forbidden by the Holy Spirit to preach the word in Asia. After they had come to Mysia, they tried to go into Bithynia, but the Spirit did not permit them. So passing by Mysia, they came down to Troas. (Acts 16:6-8)

This is Paul and his companions. They wanted to go and preach in Asia, but the Holy Spirit did not allow them to go. Paul was very in tune with the Lord, and he obeyed the Holy Spirit.

Now the Lord spoke to Paul in the night by a vision. Do not be afraid, but speak and do not keep silent; for I am with you and no one will attack you to

> hurt you; for I have many people in this city. (Acts
> 18:9-10)

Praise the Lord! Yes, if we are serving the Lord and have a close relationship with Him, He will still talk to us and guide us in our service to Him.

> And saw Him saying to me, Make haste and get out
> of Jerusalem quickly for they will not receive your
> testimony concerning Me. (Acts 22:18)

Yes, that's the Lord once again, telling Paul what to do. He does the same for us if we would just listen and obey. These next verses also speak of the Holy Spirit abiding in us to lead, guide, teach us.

> And being assembled together with them, He
> commanded them not to depart from Jerusalem, but
> to wait for the Promise of the Father, which He said,
> "you have heard from Me; for John truly baptized
> with water, but you shall be baptized with the Holy
> Spirit not many days from now. (Acts 1:4-5)

> But you shall receive power when the Holy Spirit
> has come upon you; and you shall be witnesses to
> Me in Jerusalem and in all Judea and Samaria and
> to the end of the earth. (Acts 1:8)

When the Holy Spirit dwells within us, He leads, guides, and teaches us what we need to know to be the servant that the Lord wants us to be. Are you listening, just as the prophets of the Old and the New Testaments listened?

> And I will pray the Father and He will give you
> another Helper, that He may abide with you forever.
> The Spirit of truth; whom the world cannot receive

because it neither sees Him nor knows Him; but you know Him, for He dwells with you and will be in you I will not leave you orphans, I will come to you. (John 14:16-18)

Nevertheless I tell you the truth. It is expedient for you that I go away; for if I go not away, the Comforter will not come unto you; but if I depart, I will send him unto you. (John 16:7)

However, when He, the Spirit of truth, has come, He will guide you into all truth; for He will not speak on His own authority, but whatever He hears He will speak; and He will tell you things to come. He will glorify Me, for He will take of what is Mine and declare it to you. All things that the Father has are Mine. Therefore I said that He will take of Mine and declare it to you. (John 16:13-15)

Did you understand this verse? The Holy Spirit will guide you into all truth. He will tell you what Jesus wants you to know, and Jesus will be glorified. He will take the words of Jesus and give them to you! How awesome is that!

But the anointing which you have received from Him abides in you, and you do not need that anyone teach you; but as the same anointing teaches you concerning all things, and is true, and is not a lie and just as it has taught you, you will abide in Him. (1 John 2:27)

By this we know that we abide in Him, and He in us, because He has given us of His Spirit. (1 John 4:13)

Whoever confesses that Jesus is the Son of God, God abides in him and he in God. (1 John 4:15)

> Or do you not know that your body is the temple of the Holy Spirit who is in you, whom you have from God, and you are not your own? For you were bought at a price; therefore glorify God in your body and in your spirit, which are God's. (1 Corinthians 6:19-20)

If you indeed belong to the Lord, your body is not your own. It belongs to God through the blood of Jesus, who gave His all for us, for you. This verse goes hand and hand with the following verse:

> When an unclean spirit goes out of a man he goes through dry places, seeking rest; and finding none, he says, I will return to my house from which I came. And when he comes, he finds it swept and put in order. Then he goes and takes with him seven other spirits more wicked than himself, and they enter and dwell there; and the last state of that man is worse than the first. (Luke 11:24-26)

You have to understand that the unclean spirits are Satan's demons. They indwell the bodies of people that don't have the Holy Spirit within them. If the Holy Spirit dwells in you, there isn't any room for evil demons. If someone drives out the demons, but not in the name of Jesus, and if the Holy Spirit is not within that person, the demons will return and bring with them more demons—demons that are much more wicked, and the person will be worse off. I have seen this problem with the Jehovah's Witnesses, Christian Scientists, and also in Orthodox Jewish congregations. See my chapter on spiritual warfare (chapter nine).

I will close with this very special verse, which I really like:

> So then, those who are in the flesh cannot please God. But you are not in the flesh but in the Spirit, if indeed the Spirit of God dwells in you. Now if anyone does not have the Spirit of Christ, he is not His. And if Christ is in you, the body is dead because of sin, but the Spirit is life because of righteousness. But if the Spirit of Him who raised Jesus from the dead dwells in you, He who raised Christ from the dead will also give life to your mortal bodies through His Spirit who dwells in you. (Romans 8:8-11)

Some last thoughts:

If you or anyone you know is interested in or is a part of an organized religion, I urge you to do your homework. Don't talk to anyone in that religion until you do extensive research on their beliefs. If you talk to them first, they will tell you lies and sugarcoat their unscriptural teachings!

Mormonism:

If you're interested in this religion, do research on Brigham Young's writings! He was Joseph Smith's successor. Go online and read as much as you can of Brigham Young's teachings, as well as Joseph Smith's. Then you will know for yourself what that religion teaches.

Christian Science:

Do some research on Mary Baker Eddy; she is the prophet who formed Christian Science. Read as much as you can about her and how she came about forming the organized religion. Read her teachings.

Jehovah's Witnesses:

Look into the founder, Charles Taze Russell. Read as much as you can about how he started the organized religion and what the teachings of the religion are.

Seventh Day Adventism:

Do some research on the founders: Joseph Bates, James White, Ellen G. White and J.N. Andrews. Research their teachings and their writings.

I have only listed four organized religions; there are thousands more out there. Before you enter the doors of any organized religion, do your research on the writings, beliefs, and teachings of its founders. Compare their teachings with the Word of God. Don't rely on what the members tell you. The majority of them are brainwashed, and they don't know what their founders teach. They know how to tell you what you want to hear to get you to come into the religion. They will talk about Jesus, but not the Jesus of the Gospels. Be very careful!

I have given many Scriptures throughout this book, but I'm not saying that I necessarily chose the best Scriptures. The entire Bible is full of fantastic Scriptures to use. I would like to encourage you to seek out other Scriptures for yourselves and to live by them your entire life. Use them to serve the Lord wherever He will lead you.

> I pray that this book was an encouragement for you, and that you will stay strong and focused upon serving our almighty God. Let Him be the reason that you live: the reason your heart beats, the reason you breathe. There is a song that I would like to quote a few lines from: I believe that is the way

the saint should live their lives. The song is called
"Kingdom Come" by Damaris:

Let your vision be my vision
Let your dream be my dream
Let your passion be my passion
Let your mission be my mission

I believe this should be the prayer of every saint; we
should want to serve the Lord, to be used by Him
as His puppet on a string for Him to use us for His
purpose for His will to be done through us.

We are to live our lives not for what pleases us, but only to strive
to capture the heart of Jesus through our services to Him.

May our Lord and Savior bless you and your service to Him.